Folens

Starlight

The Complete Primary English Programme

4th Class

Combined Reading & Skills Book

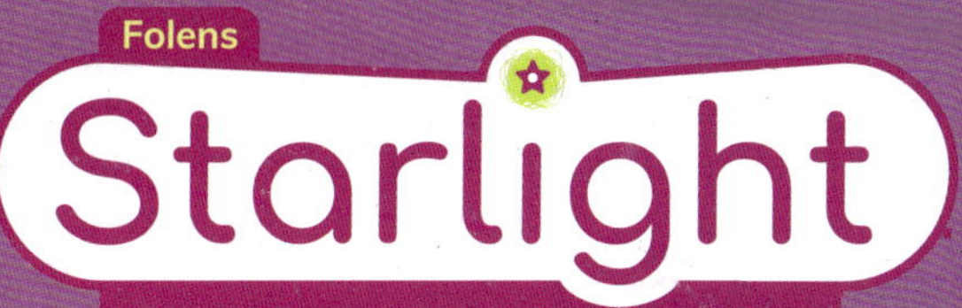

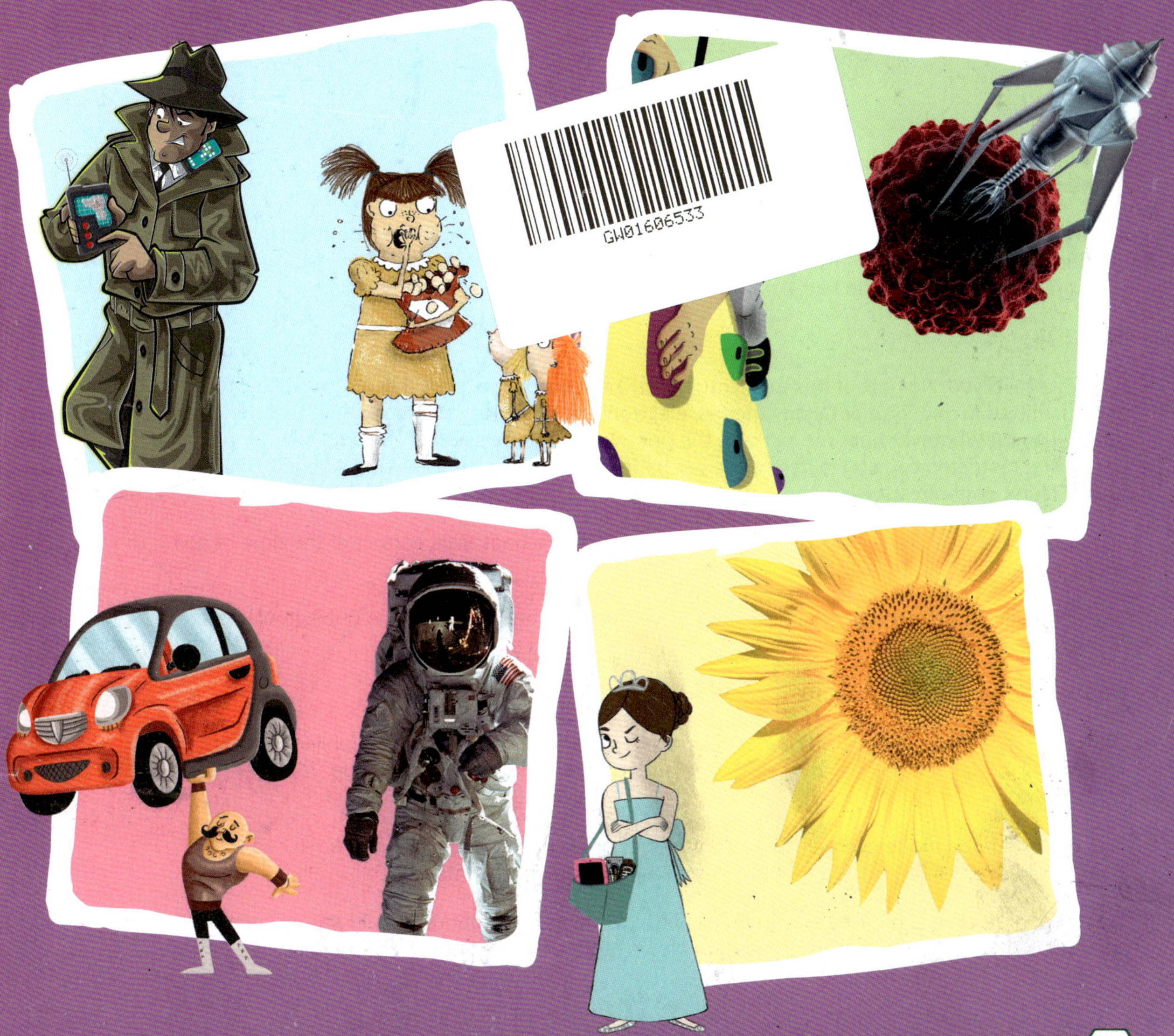

FOLENS

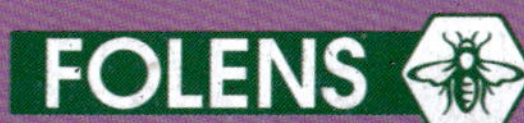

Starlight is a comprehensive English language programme that is aligned to the 2015 Primary Language Curriculum. Every unit is centred around a genre and theme so that each of the three curriculum strands – Oral language, Reading and Writing – can be taught in a completely integrated way.

The Combined Reading and Skills Books for Third–Sixth Class each contain 16 units designed to last two weeks. Each unit consists of two texts and accompanying activities and the following genres are covered: Recount, Report, Procedure, Narrative, Explanation, Persuasive and Poetry. The texts are all high-interest topics that will greatly appeal to children. The activities focus on literal and inferential comprehension, vocabulary development, grammar and writing development.

First published in 2019 by Folens Publishers

Hibernian Industrial Estate, Greenhills Road, Tallaght, Dublin 24

Author: Catherine Baker

Illustrations: Beehive Illustration Agency: Adam Linley, Joseph Wilkins. The Bright Agency: David Shephard, Erin Taylor, James Rey Sanchez, Jeff Crowther, Laura Watkins, Marina Martin, Nan Lawson, Pauline Reeves, Ria Lee; Andrew Painter.

ISBN 9781-7892-7016-7

Photograph acknowledgements

Alamy; Getty; Science Photo Library; Shutterstock; p. 61 Tristan McConnell, supplied by Tristan McConnell; p. 62 Eimear O'Grady, supplied by Independent News and Media; pp. 116–118, supplied by Trócaire.

Contents

1a The Race to Space

During the Second World War, the United States of America and the Soviet Union were on the same side. They fought together against Germany. But the two countries didn't really trust each other. In fact, they were more like enemies than friends. Each country thought that the other wanted to control the world.

Leader of the Soviet Union, Joseph Stalin, with US President Franklin D. Roosevelt

Nuclear bomb test

After the Second World War ended in 1945, some people thought that the USA and the Soviet Union might go to war against each other. Both countries started to develop powerful new weapons. They created and tested new types of bombs. Many people worried that they would use these new weapons in a war. Fortunately, that didn't happen. However, the USA and the Soviet Union kept on **competing** to prove they were the best in other ways.

Both countries wanted to be the first to send rockets into space. In October 1957 the Soviet Union **launched** a **satellite** called *Sputnik 1* into space. It was just a small metal sphere about the size of a beach ball. But it made the Americans very worried indeed. It showed that the Soviet Union was becoming better than the USA at developing **technology**.

Sputnik 1

Sputnik 1 **orbited** the Earth for 21 days. Just a month later, the Soviets launched *Sputnik 2* with a dog called Laika on board. Laika was the first living creature ever to go into space. She was trained to eat a special gel that would be her food during the mission. Laika orbited the Earth for two days. This proved that living things could survive in space.

Laika, the first dog in space

Humans in space

Yuri Gagarin

The Soviets kept on developing new satellites. In 1959 a space **probe** called *Luna 3* was launched. It successfully took the first photographs of the dark side of the moon!

In April 1961, Soviet astronaut Yuri Gagarin became the first person to orbit the Earth. He did this in a tiny spacecraft called *Vostok 1*.

The Soviets were the first to send a human being into space. But the Americans weren't far behind. Just one month later, Alan Shepard became the first American in space. However, his flight only lasted about 15 minutes. In February 1962 John Glenn was the first American to orbit the Earth.

Alan Shepard

Next stop – the Moon

The real **challenge** was to be the first to get a human on the Moon. Both sides were **desperate** to achieve this. In 1961 the American President, John F. Kennedy, started the *Apollo* programme. It had one clear aim – to land a man on the Moon by the end of the **decade**. The Soviets had the same **intention**. But only one side could win this race.

John F. Kennedy announces the *Apollo* programme

On 16 July 1969 three American **astronauts** set off into space. Their names were Neil Armstrong, Edwin 'Buzz' Aldrin and Michael Collins and their goal was to land on the Moon. The whole world was watching as the *Apollo* spacecraft lifted off. Four days later, Armstrong and Aldrin landed on the surface of the Moon. As he stepped onto the Moon, Neil Armstrong said, 'One small step for man, one giant leap for mankind.' This **announced** to the world that the Americans had won the space race.

From left to right: Neil Armstrong, Michael Collins and Buzz Aldrin

Buzz Aldrin walks on the Moon. This photo was taken by Neil Armstrong.

A. Comprehension: Fact finding

Answer the questions.

1. Who did the USA and Soviet Union fight in the Second World War?
2. Which country was first to send a satellite into space?
3. Who was Laika?
4. What did Yuri Gagarin do?
5. What was 'Buzz' Aldrin's real first name?

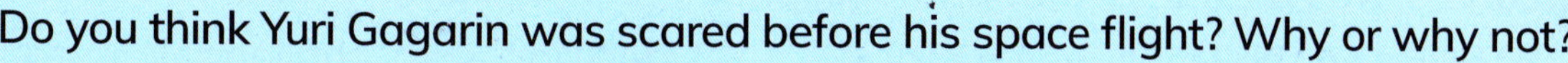

Do you think Yuri Gagarin was scared before his space flight? Why or why not?

B. Comprehension: Read between the lines

Answer the questions.

1. Why did people think the USA and Soviet Union might fight?
2. What did Laika's orbit prove?
3. What was the purpose of the Apollo programme?
4. How might Americans have felt as they watched the Moon landing?
5. What does 'one small step for man, one giant leap for mankind' mean?

Why do you think the USA wanted to be first on the Moon?

C. Vocabulary

Choose the word or phrase that is nearest in meaning to the underlined word or phrase.

1. Stephen and Femi were competing for first place.
   a) fighting **b)** comparing **c)** sprinting **d)** preparing
2. Jane was desperate to be chosen for the school play.
   a) sad **b)** longing **c)** first **d)** disappointed
3. My oldest cousin is a decade older than me.
   a) ten years **b)** one month **c)** a few years **d)** ten months
4. It wasn't my intention to make Megan cry.
   a) dream **b)** fault **c)** aim **d)** game
5. The early astronauts had to be very brave.
   a) scientists **b)** space travellers **c)** pilots **d)** astronomers
6. Mr Molloy announced a fantastic new writing competition.
   a) awarded **b)** told everyone about **c)** set up **d)** cancelled

Put these words into sentences: intention, astronauts, announced.

D. Vocabulary

Choose the most suitable word to complete each sentence.

1. After the countdown, the rocket was _______ into space. (launched, orbited, announced)
2. A _______ can orbit Earth or another planet. (satellite, space, star)
3. It took a lot of new _______ to reach the Moon. (time, technology, space)
4. The rocket _______ the Moon. (journeyed, sailed, orbited)
5. *Luna 3* was a _______ that photographed the Moon. (star, probe, astronaut)
6. Landing on the Moon was a real _______. (decision, sum, challenge)

Write a dictionary definition for one of the words you chose.

E. Grammar: Capital letters (part 1)

We use **capital letters** for:

CAPITAL LETTERS

The start of a sentence	**Example:** Trolls are huge, but not clever.
The word 'I'	**Example:** When **I** laugh, my eyes water.
Names of people, places and animals	**Examples:** Neil Armstrong, Paris, Laika.
Days of the week, months and special days	**Examples:** Monday, July, Christmas Day.

Write the sentences, adding capital letters where they are needed.

1. my birthday is in march.
2. i got my rabbit, mindy, last saturday.
3. amy and jason went away to italy.
4. mrs hedges used to live in america.
5. it was snowing in dublin on christmas eve.
6. on sunday we went to the cinema in galway.

Write the sentences, adding words with capital letters to fill the gaps.

1. My birthday is in the month of _______.
2. _______ is my favourite day of the week.
3. If I could go to any country in the world, I would visit _______.
4. _______ was the first person to walk on the Moon.
5. I like going to my friend _______'s house.
6. I often visit the town of _______ during the summer.

Write a sentence about a holiday, using capital letters in three different ways.

F. Writing skills: Time words and phrases

In a recount, we use **time words and phrases** to tell the reader the order in which things happened. **Examples:** first, during, later, in 2018.

Choose the correct time words and phrases to fill the gaps.

in 1969 first then after a while on 11 November 2011

1. Emma wanted to stay up, but _______ she was too tired to keep her eyes open.
2. _______, Neil Armstrong and Buzz Aldrin landed on the Moon.
3. _______ we went to the museum, and _______ we got ice cream.
4. President Michael D. Higgins was elected _______.

Read the text below.

I had a strange dream last night. First, I was an astronaut, travelling to a far away planet. When I arrived, I met an alien. At first I couldn't understand him, but I eventually figured out his language. During our conversation, he kept licking his lips. After a while, I realised that he wanted to eat me! I woke up then!

1. Make a list of all the time words and phrases you can find in the story.
2. Write sentences for three of the time words and phrases in your list.

G. Writing genre: Planning a recount

A **recount** is a retelling of a past experience or event. A recount:

- Begins with an **opening**, saying **who** it is about, and **where** and **when** it took place
- Can be **real or imagined**
- Is written in the **past tense** with events in **chronological order**
- Uses **time words and phrases**
- **Concludes** with the writer's opinion.

Plan a recount.

1. Choose one of the missions below. Use books or the internet to research it.
   - ★ The Apollo 13 mission to the Moon
   - ★ The Mars Rover *Opportunity*'s journey to Mars.
2. Fill in the table in your copy with notes for writing your recount.

Opening: who, where and when?	What happened? Write it in order.	Conclusion: what was your opinion of the event?
	Event 1, Event 2, Event 3...	

1b Valentina Tereshkova: First Woman in Space

You have probably heard of the first men to set foot on the Moon: Americans Neil Armstrong and Buzz Aldrin. But you might not know the story of the Soviet astronaut (or cosmonaut) Valentina Tereshkova. She was the first woman ever to go into space and orbit the Earth.

Early life

Tereshkova was born on 6 March 1937 in a village in the Soviet Union. When she was only two years old, her father was killed fighting in the Second World War. Her mother took a job in a local factory so she could afford to look after Tereshkova and her brother and sister.

When she was 16, Tereshkova left school to work in the factory too.

As a teenager, Tereshkova joined a **parachute** club. It was her interest in parachuting that **eventually** got her into space!

Soviet Space Centre, Star City

Joining the space race

Tereshkova made over 120 parachute jumps with the club. During this time, she also became interested in space. In 1961 the astronauts Gherman Titov and Yuri Gagarin were launched into space. Valentina thought it would be wonderful to orbit the Earth just like them. So she **applied** to the Soviet Space Centre at Star City.

Tereshkova picked a good time to **volunteer**. The Soviets were looking for new ways of beating the United States in the space race. So they were keen to be first to put a woman into space. Cosmonauts at the time also had to parachute from their capsules before they hit the ground. So Tereshkova's parachuting experience made her a good fit.

Valentina Tereshkova undergoing tough training exercises for space

Tereshkova was asked to go Moscow for a **medical** examination and an **interview**. Along with four other women, she passed! All five women began training as astronauts.

The women **trainees** went through the same training as the men. There were tough exercises to help them survive space travel. But Tereshkova was very **persistent**. She had the right **attitude** and the right abilities. In the end, she was the only one of the five women who made it into space. On 16 June 1963 she went into orbit in *Vostok 6*. As the spacecraft took off, she shouted: 'Hey, sky, take off your hat! I'm on my way!'

Tereshkova's space flight

Tereshkova's flight on *Vostok 6* lasted just under three days. During the flight, she orbited Earth 48 times. Valentina's flight was a long one. The four American astronauts who came before her only made 36 orbits between them.

On her return, Tereshkova had to parachute from a height of over 6000 m above Earth! She landed safely in central Asia. The local people welcomed her by inviting her to dinner! She was given the title of Hero of the Soviet Union, in **recognition** of her bravery.

Later life

Valentina Tereshkova never went back into space. However, she **represented** the Soviet Union abroad many times. She even had a crater on the Moon named after her! She married another astronaut, Andrian Nikolayev. Their daughter, Yelena, was the first baby whose parents had both been into space.

Tereshkova made history with her space flight. It was almost 20 years before another female astronaut went into space. Valentina Tereshkova was a true **pioneer**.

A. Comprehension: Fact finding

Answer the questions.

1. What happened when Tereshkova was two years old?
2. Where did Tereshkova work when she left school?
3. Who inspired Tereshkova to apply for astronaut training?
4. What was the name of Tereshkova's spacecraft?
5. What was unusual about Tereshkova's daughter, Yelena?

Which fact about Tereshkova do you find most interesting? Why?

B. Comprehension: Read between the lines

Answer the questions.

1. Why might Tereshkova be less famous than Armstrong and Aldrin?
2. How did Tereshkova's parachuting help her to become an astronaut?
3. Why did the Soviet Union want to send a woman into space?
4. Describe Tereshkova's personality in your own words.
5. 'Valentina Tereshkova was a true pioneer.' Do you agree? Why or why not?

How do you think Tereshkova felt when she landed back on Earth?

C. Vocabulary

Choose the word or phrase that is nearest in meaning to the underlined word.

1. I <u>applied</u> to join a judo club.
   a) didn't want **b)** requested **c)** refused **d)** hoped
2. Mam had an <u>interview</u> before she got the job.
   a) meeting **b)** excuse **c)** opportunity **d)** accident
3. You need to be <u>persistent</u> if you want to succeed.
   a) wise **b)** old **c)** clever **d)** determined
4. Tereshkova deserves <u>recognition</u> for her achievement.
   a) help **b)** happiness **c)** refusal **d)** appreciation
5. Valentina Tereshkova <u>represented</u> the Soviet Union.
   a) ignored **b)** insulted **c)** stood for **d)** encouraged
6. The <u>pioneer</u> was first to reach the distant land.
   a) traveller **b)** trailblazer **c)** hard worker **d)** politician

Write a sentence about Tereshkova, using 'persistent' and 'recognition'.

D. Vocabulary

Choose the most suitable word to complete each sentence.

eventually volunteer medical trainee parachute attitude

1. Dan is not the fastest runner, but he has a positive ________.
2. I wanted to ________ to raise money for charity.
3. When you jump out of a plane, you need a ________.
4. The ________ pilot was nervous about his first solo flight.
5. Would-be astronauts need to have a ________ examination.
6. If you are persistent, you will succeed ________.

Write sentences for two of the words from the box.

E. Grammar: Capital letters (part 2)

Remember: we use **capital letters** at the beginning of a sentence, for the pronoun 'I', for the names of people and places, and for days of the week, months and special days.

Write the paragraph using capital letters.

last sunday was a very unusual day. as well as being easter sunday, it was also cian's birthday. we all got easter eggs, and cian got some cool presents. he was a bit disappointed because really he wanted a dog. then mam said she had a surprise for him. we all got in the car and went to a house in castlebar where they had a dog and some tiny puppies. cian was delighted because mam let him choose one! we are going to call it conan.

Write sentences about the subjects below. Don't forget capital letters!

1. Your favourite month of the year.
2. The city, town or village where you live.
3. Your favourite singer.
4. What you would call a pet panda, if you had one.
5. A good friend.
6. A country you would like to visit.

Write two sentences about Valentina Tereshkova's space flight. Make sure you use capital letters correctly.

F. Writing skills: Formal and informal language

Use **informal language** when writing to or chatting with a friend.
Example: Ever heard of those guys who were on the Moon?
Use more **formal language** to give information clearly and accurately.
Example: You may have heard of the first men to reach the Moon.
Recounts about historical events normally use formal language.

Write which sentence in each pair is formal or informal.

1. (a) There's no way you should have to put up with bullying and stuff.
   (b) Do not suffer the unpleasant effects of bullying.
2. (a) Do not panic if you see a stag beetle; they are large, but not dangerous.
   (b) If you spot a stag beetle, stay cool – they look scary, but won't hurt you!
3. (a) Astronauts must train hard and remain in peak fitness.
   (b) Wanna be a space guy or girl? Wow, you'd better be fit!

Write the text using more formal language.

Tons of kids are dying to be astronauts, but only the best of the bunch get picked. You need to be a bit of a nerd and super fit. If you're an exercise nut AND brainy, who knows? You just might make it.

G. Writing genre: Writing a recount

Use the notes you made in Unit 1a to write a recount about a space mission.

1. Remember to:
   - Start with an opening that says **who** the recount is about, and **where** and **when** it took place.
   - Tell the reader about each event in **chronological order**.
   - Use **formal language**.
   - Add a **conclusion**, giving your opinion of the event.
2. When you are finished, reread your work and correct any mistakes.

2a Nanotechnology: It's a Small World!

Introduction

'Nano' comes from *nanos*, the **ancient** Greek word for 'dwarf'. That should give you a clue about what nanotechnology is. It involves making very tiny things from parts the size of **atoms**. Since atoms are the smallest **particles** of a substance, that's very small indeed. It is incredible that scientists can make things out of single atoms.

Can you imagine being as small as an atom? If you were the size of a **carbon** atom, a **regular** ant would be 10 million times bigger than you!

Eeek!

Nanofact

In maths, 'nano' means 'one-billionth'. So a nanometre is one-billionth of a metre. An ant that is 3 mm long, measures 3 million nanometres! Nanometres are useful for measuring objects like atoms ... but not really for ants!

Small but strong!

The **substance** carbon exists in different **forms**. One form is the 'lead' in your pencil. This form of carbon is quite soft. Another form is diamond. This form is extremely hard. The difference is because of the way the carbon atoms join together.

In 1985, a new form of carbon was discovered. Scientists realised that it was very light but very strong. They found they could arrange the carbon atoms into different shapes. One of these shapes was a cylinder, which they called a nanotube. A nanotube can be 300 times stronger than steel.

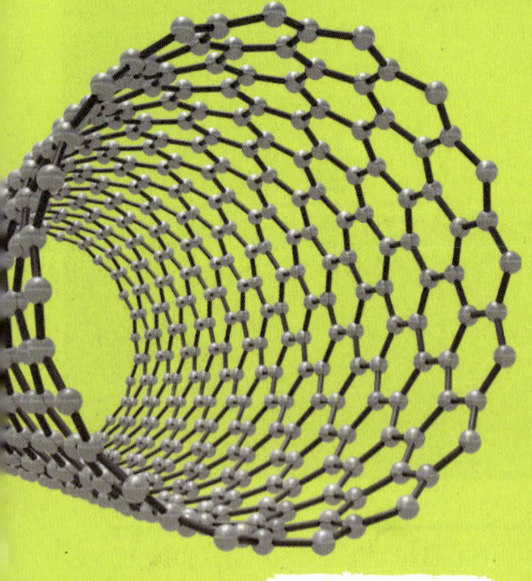

A nanotube

Harnessing nano-power

It's not easy for humans to create things from tiny atoms. Single atoms are far too small to see with our eyes, or hold with our fingers. Luckily, scientists have invented some very powerful new **microscopes**. These let people see an image of things as small as atoms. They even allow people to move single atoms around. This helps us learn about the extremely tiny world of atoms and how we can **harness** it. And then we can create new **inventions**, using nanotechnology.

Nanotechnology in our world

Nanotechnology will do some amazing things in the future. But there are many examples of nanotechnology in our world already. You might even have some in your socks! Here are some of the ways that we are already using nanotechnology.

This 'drinkable book' is made of special paper that can filter water.

- **Nanoparticles** are used in sunscreen nowadays. These tiny particles are more effective at blocking the Sun's rays than the material in older sunscreens.
- New types of **fabric** have nano-sized whiskers. These whiskers help to keep water out of your clothes so you don't get wet in the rain.
- Silver nanoparticles are very good at killing off the **bacteria** that make your feet smelly. That's why they are sometimes used in socks.
- Silver nanoparticles can also be used in special paper to **filter** dirty water. This makes the water safe to drink.
- Nanotechnology is also being used in some new medicines. Nanoparticles can carry tiny amounts of special drugs to individual cells, to help defeat diseases such as cancer.

Nanofact

Nanoparticles are very tiny particles of different substances. They are usually 100 nanometers or less in size and can be used in nanotechnology.

The nanofuture

Nanotechnology is already used to create very light but strong materials. Soon these materials will be used instead of metal to make lighter cars. The lighter a car is, the less fuel it uses. Since **fossil fuels** are bad for the **environment**, nanotechnology could even help us solve some of the problems of climate change.

Scientists are also working on tiny machines, such as motors and robots. In the future, it may be possible to send these nanomachines into the human body. They might be able to carry out repairs on organs, or even find and destroy cancer cells.

An artist's impression of nanomachines inside the human body

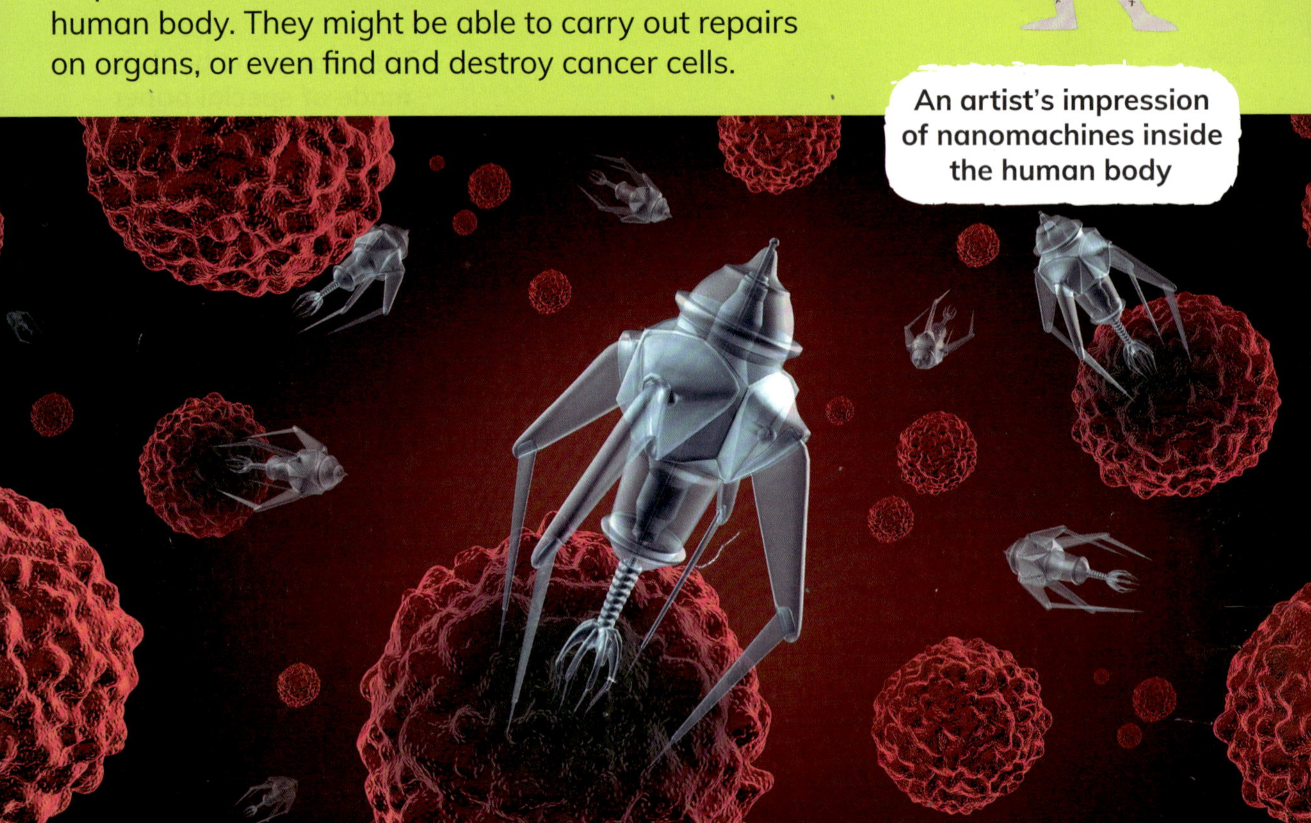

Conclusion

Nanotechnology is making a real difference in our world today. But the future of nanotechnology looks even more exciting. It is likely we will find many other uses for this exciting technology. It's a small world with huge **possibilities**.

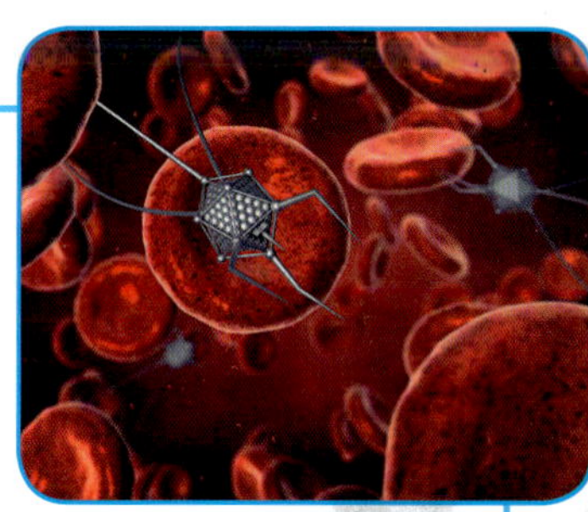

A. Comprehension: Fact finding

Answer the questions.

1. What does 'nanos' mean in Ancient Greek?
2. What are atoms?
3. What is a nanotube?
4. What nanoparticle might you have in your socks? Why?
5. How is nanotechnology already being used in medicine?

Name one good thing nanotechnology might do in the future.

B. Comprehension: Read between the lines

Answer the questions.

1. Why aren't nanometres useful for measuring larger objects?
2. How have special microscopes helped develop nanotechnology?
3. List three facts you learned from this report.
4. Which do you think is the most interesting section of the report? Why?
5. Imagine you could do something with nanotechnology. What would it be?

Find one fact and one opinion in the Introduction section of the text.

C. Vocabulary

Choose the word or phrase that is nearest in meaning to the underlined word.

1. Many English words come from <u>ancient</u> languages.
   a) similar **b)** well-known **c)** unknown **d)** very old
2. Cooking apples are not as sweet as <u>regular</u> apples.
   a) unusual **b)** boring **c)** small **d)** normal
3. Water and ice are the same <u>substance</u> in different forms.
   a) food **b)** material **c)** liquid **d)** idea
4. Scientists have <u>harnessed</u> the power of nanotechnology.
   a) invented **b)** helped **c)** used **d)** felt
5. Nanotechnology has made lots of cool <u>inventions</u> possible.
   a) new creations **b)** ideas **c)** medicines **d)** nanoparticles
6. Some <u>bacteria</u> can make you ill.
   a) scientists **b)** germs **c)** foods **d)** minibeasts

Write about an imaginary invention, using two of the underlined words.

D. Vocabulary

Choose the most suitable word to complete each sentence.

1. Nanometres are good for measuring ______. (people, ants, atoms)
2. A ______ is a very small piece of something. (bacterium, particle, medicine)
3. ______ is an element found in things such as charcoal. (carbon, clay, bacteria)
4. Scientists use ______ to see the nanoparticles. (bacteria, atoms, microscopes)
5. Tiny ______ are used in nanotechnology. (nanoparticles, carbons, microscopes)
6. Many scientists try to protect the ______. (life, environment, empire)

Can you think of any other words that start with 'micro'?

E. Grammar: Capital letters and end punctuation (part 1)

Sentences always begin with a **capital letter**.
All sentences must end with:
A **question mark (?)** for a question. **Example:** How old are you?
An **exclamation mark (!)** for strong feelings. **Example:** I won!
A **full stop (.)** at the end of most other sentences.

Write the sentences. Add the correct end punctuation.

1. Have you ever seen a goblin
2. I went on a picnic with Beth and Ted
3. I can't believe you just said that
4. Mr Murphy's tie is on fire
5. Is it time for the party yet
6. I've eaten all my packed lunch

Write the sentences with capital letters and end punctuation.

1. i'd like to see my cousin jake more often, but he lives in london
2. have you ever met a dog as daft as barney
3. 'surprise' said megan. 'i've bought you a pet armadillo'
4. sean says he saw a dragon outside
5. it rained all day on wednesday, but we still went to wicklow
6. would you like to spend christmas on the beach in sydney, australia

Find sentences ending in ! and ? on page 18.

F. Writing skills: Using subheadings

Subheadings divide up information into chunks. Clear subheadings can help the reader find particular information.

Look again at the report *Nanotechnology: It's a Small World!*

- Write a list of the subheadings.
- Choose one of the sections and think of a new subheading for it.

Read the text below.

Some of the smallest animals on Earth live in water! The smallest adult fish ever found is called Paedocypris and it's less than a centimetre long. Paedocypris lives in swamps and streams in South East Asia. Some very tiny animals live in sea water too. Plankton are minute animals and plants that drift in the sea. They are a good source of food for larger animals – including massive ones like the basking shark.

1. Write the text, starting a new paragraph when the topic changes.
2. Write a subheading for each paragraph.

G. Writing genre: Using a KWL chart to plan a report

Reports normally contain lots of facts. A **KWL chart** helps you research facts and plan your writing.

Plan a report about very tiny or very large animals using a KWL chart.

1. Create a KWL chart like the one below.

What I Know	What I Want to Know	What I Have Learned
The blue whale is the largest animal in the world.	What is the largest animal that lives on land?	The African elephant

2. Write what you know about your topic in the **K** column.
3. Write all the things you want to know in the **W** column.
4. Use books and the internet to research the answers to your questions. Write the answers in the **L** column.

Group your facts into paragraphs. Think of a subheading for each paragraph.

2b Build It Big!

Introduction

All throughout history, people have tried to **construct** buildings that are as tall as possible. Sometimes they did this to **honour** gods or to create places of **worship**. But sometimes it was because humans like a challenge! For a very long time, it was hard to create very tall buildings. The **sophisticated** building **techniques** we use today have made it easy to build huge **skyscrapers**. Builders in the past didn't have our techniques or our modern tools. This makes the **structures** they created even more amazing!

The ancient world

Ancient Egyptian **pharaohs** were buried inside **impressive** pyramids. The tallest of all is the Great Pyramid of Giza. This was built around 4,500 years ago and it stands 147 m tall. That's nearly twice as big as the tallest building in the Republic of Ireland, the Elysian in Cork!

Middle Ages

Later, in the Middle Ages, **craftsmen** and builders competed to build very tall churches. The Great Pyramid was the tallest building in the world for over 3,000 years. Then, in 1311, a huge cathedral was built in the city of Lincoln, England. Lincoln Cathedral probably reached a height of about 160 m. No one knows its height for sure, though. Unfortunately, the tallest **spire collapsed** in 1549, during a terrible storm.

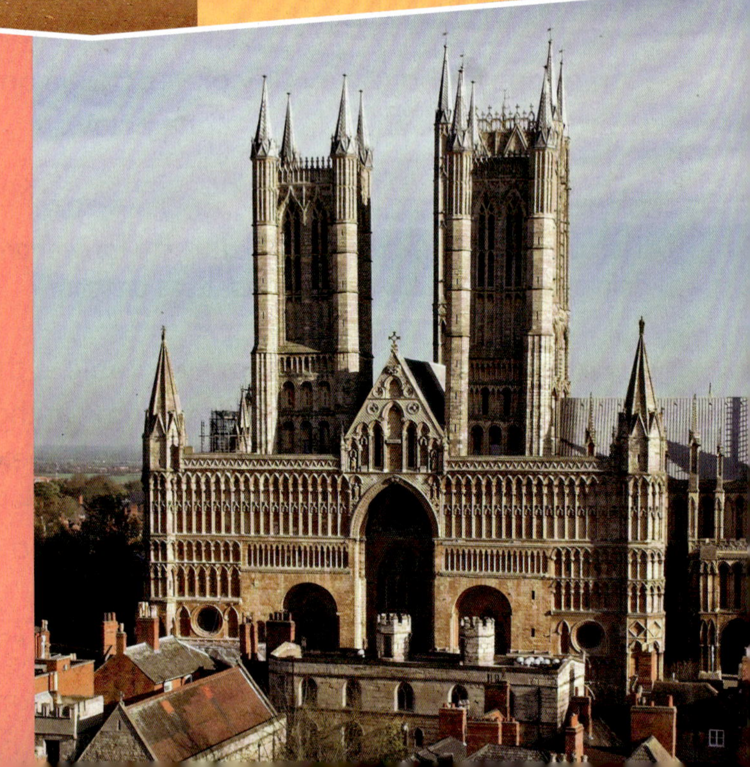

The 1800s

The record of Lincoln Cathedral stood for a long time. But in the 1800s, several very tall structures were built.

The Washington Monument stands in the city of Washington DC in the United States. It was built to honour the first US president, George Washington. It's in the shape of an **obelisk** – a tall column of stone. It was built in 1848. At 169 m tall, it's taller than Lincoln Cathedral ever was.

What do you imagine when you think of Paris? It's probably the **iconic** shape of the Eiffel Tower. This amazing building was completed in 1889. The main building is 300 m tall. It's a stunning building to look at and to climb up. No wonder it gets nearly seven million visitors a year!

The twentieth century

As building techniques got more **sophisticated**, taller buildings became possible.

The Chrysler Building in New York was built in 1930. At 319 m, it was even taller than the Eiffel Tower. But its record only lasted 11 months. Amazingly, though, it's still the world's tallest brick building.

The building that stole the Chrysler's crown as world's tallest building was the Empire State Building, also in New York. Built in 1931, it is 381 m high.

As the twentieth century went on, more and more tall buildings were constructed. The Empire State Building was smaller than the Ostankino Tower in Moscow, Russia. This measured 537 m and it's still the tallest structure in Europe. It was built to broadcast TV signals.

Bringing it up to date

The CN Tower in Toronto, Canada, was the tallest building from 1975 up until 2007. It is 553 m tall. If you've got a really good head for heights, you could visit the CN Tower. You can even do an 'edge walk' around the outside of the tower, 356 m above street level.

So what's the tallest building in the world right now? The building that took over from the CN Tower was the Burj Khalifa in Dubai. It was completed in 2010. This gigantic skyscraper measures an enormous 830 m! But the race is already on to beat it. The Jeddah Tower in Saudi Arabia is due to complete in about 2020. If all goes to plan, it will be 1000 m – (1 km) – tall!

Whatever next?

However tall it is, the Jeddah Tower probably won't be the world's tallest building forever. People will always want to build bigger, stronger, taller towers. And with new technology, it's getting easier. How high is it possible to build a tower? Maybe the sky's the limit!

A. Comprehension: Fact finding

Answer the questions.

1. What is the name of the tallest Egyptian pyramid?
2. How tall is the Washington Monument?
3. For how long was the Chrysler Building the world's tallest building?
4. What is the Chrysler Building's claim to fame today?
5. What is the tallest structure in Europe used for?

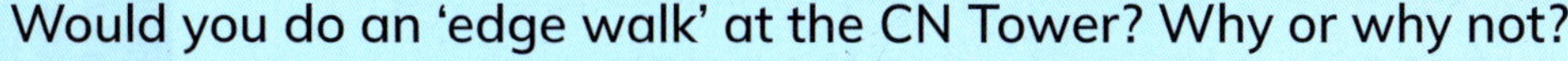

Would you do an 'edge walk' at the CN Tower? Why or why not?

B. Comprehension: Read between the lines

Answer the questions.

1. Why are people still trying to build taller buildings?
2. Why were the Egyptian pharaohs buried inside impressive pyramids?
3. Why are there more tall towers now than in the Middle Ages?
4. Why can't we tell how tall Lincoln Cathedral was originally?
5. In what way did the Empire State Building 'steal the Chrysler's crown'?

Which of the buildings would you most like to visit? Why?

C. Vocabulary

Choose the word or phrase that is nearest in meaning to the underlined word.

1. We used branches to construct a den in the woods.
   a) build **b)** destroy **c)** imagine **d)** invent
2. In art class, we make pictures using different techniques.
   a) paints **b)** materials **c)** methods **d)** ideas
3. The pyramids were smaller structures than skyscrapers.
   a) tombs **b)** buildings **c)** statues **d)** objects
4. The Burj Khalifa is a very impressive building.
   a) tall **b)** recent **c)** unusual **d)** remarkable
5. Dad's old shed collapsed when there was a bad storm.
   a) fell down **b)** blew away **c)** leaked **d)** stood strong
6. Some buildings, like the Eiffel Tower, are iconic.
   a) tall **b)** recognisable **c)** ancient **d)** unfamiliar

Write about a famous building using 'impressive'.

D. Vocabulary

Choose the most suitable word to complete each sentence.

worship   skyscrapers   pharaohs   craftsmen   honour   sophisticated

1. Builders use ______ technology to build very high towers.
2. The rulers of ancient Egypt were called ______.
3. Many people ______ in churches, mosques and synagogues.
4. If you go to New York you will see many tall ______.
5. In the Middle Ages, cathedrals were built by skilled ______.
6. Statues are often put up to ______ famous people.

Write sentences using 'worship' and 'honour'.

E. Grammar: Capital letters and end punctuation (part 2)

Remember: sentences begin with a **capital letter** and end with a **question mark (?)**, **exclamation mark (!)** or **full stop (.)**.

Write the story with correct capital letters and end punctuation.

last summer we went camping during the holidays? the first morning, i woke up very early! mam and Dad were still asleep. I shook my brother patrick to wake him up. 'quick' i said. 'Why don't we go exploring'

'Go away, cara' patrick groaned. 'I'm asleep.' So I crept out of the tent without him.

it was chilly outside the tent, but there was a beautiful sunrise? I stood there for a while, watching it. all of a sudden i saw something amazing. a deer came out of the nearby wood and looked straight at me?

Write the paragraph. Add capital letters and end punctuation.

the custom house is located on the banks of the river liffey in dublin it was built in 1781 by an english architect called james gandon it cost £200,000 to build which was extremely expensive for the time have you ever visited the custom house would you like to see it

Write three sentences. End each one with a different type of punctuation.

F. Writing skills: Paragraphs

A **paragraph** is a group of sentences about the same idea. We start a new paragraph for:

- A new subject
- A shift in time
- A change in place.

Reread page 25 and complete the activities below.

1. Find a place where a new paragraph starts.
2. Write the first sentence of the new paragraph.
3. Explain *why* the author changed to a new paragraph there.

Write the text, including a paragraph break.

Some people believe that a massive prehistoric monster lives in the waters of Loch Ness in Scotland. People have claimed that they've seen 'Nessie', the monster. However, no sightings have ever been proven. In Ireland in the nineteenth century, a similar monster to Nessie was spotted off the coast of Co. Clare. This was a strange and frightening sea monster with a long tail and a head that looked like a horse.

G. Writing genre: Writing a report

Use the KWL chart you made in Unit 2a to write a report about very tiny or very large animals.

1. Think of a good title for your report.
2. Write your report, remembering to break it into paragraphs.
3. Write a clear subheading for each paragraph.
4. When you are finished, check your work using the checklist below:
   - Is your report clear and easy to understand?
   - Have you used formal language?
   - Could you put any of your facts into a fact box?
   - Could you include any images or diagrams?
5. Write a second draft of your report, making any improvements that are needed.

3a How to Play Rounders

Rounders is a **versatile** game that's easy to play and lots of fun. You can play it at school, with a club or even just in the park with your friends. It's a bat-and-ball game for two teams of players. One team's players hit a ball with the bat and then **attempt** to run around four bases. The other team's players are the fielders – their job is to **retrieve** the ball.

Here are some basic instructions for how to play rounders.

Aim

To score 'runs' by running all the way around the bases. The winning team is the one with the most rounders (runs) at the end.

What you need

- An open area, like a football field
- Five squares of carpet or cardboard. These will be the four bases and the pitcher's stand. You can use coats or jumpers instead if you're playing in the park!
- A bat and ball
- Two teams of up to nine players each
- A referee (unless you're just playing for fun).

What to do

Setting up

First, set up the bases so the pitch looks like this diagram.

The four bases go in a square. There are about 30 strides between each base.

The pitcher's stand goes about 13 strides away from the batter's box.

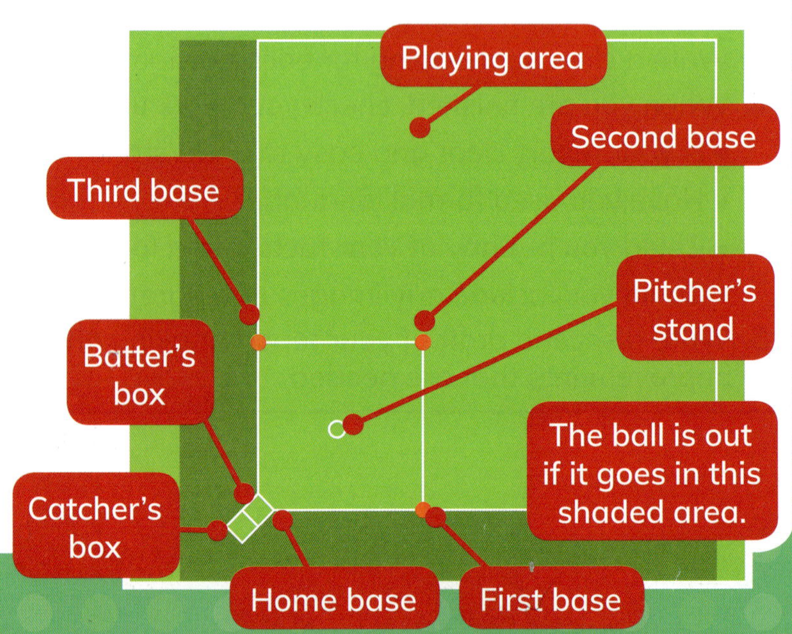

Next, decide which team will be the first fielding team and which will be the first batting and running team.

Rules for the fielding team

The nine fielders stand in these positions.

- The pitcher (or bowler) stands 13 strides from the batter's box.
- The short stop stands just behind the pitcher, to the pitcher's right.
- The catcher stands behind the batter's box.
- One fielder stands at first base, one at second base and one at third base.
- Two fielders stand further out between second and third base.
- One fielder stands further out between first and second base.

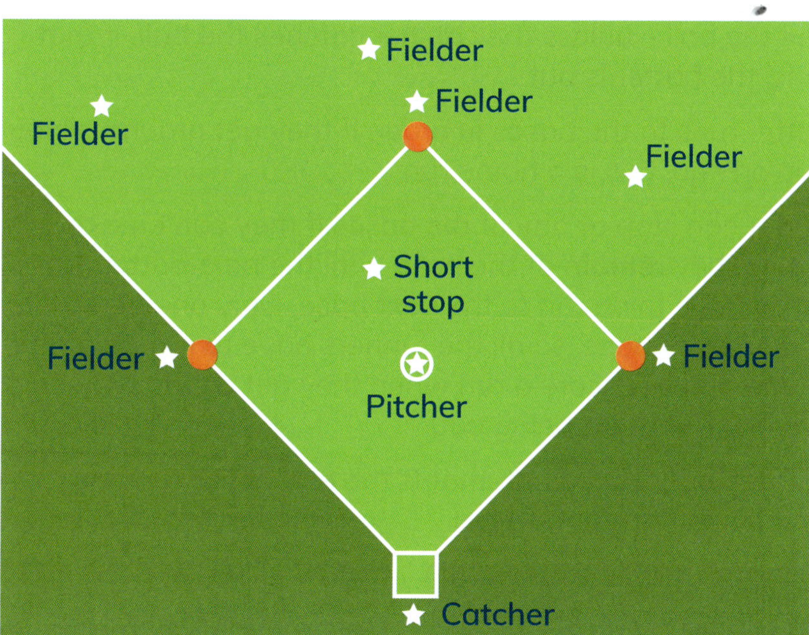

It's the fielders' job to try to get the batter and the runners out.
The batter is out if:

- They don't hit the ball, and the catcher catches it
- They hit the ball and it is caught by a fielder before it bounces
- A fielder is holding the ball and tags the batter or another runner between two bases
- A fielder gets the ball to a base before the batter or another runner reaches it.

Runners are out if they are running towards a base and a fielder gets there first with the ball.

Rules for the batting and running team

- All players get the **opportunity** to bat.
- The referee calls up the batters in turn.
- The batter stands in the batter's box, by home base.
- The pitcher throws the ball towards the catcher, who stands behind the batter.
- The batter must try to hit the ball and stop the catcher from catching it.
- Each batter gets up to three goes at hitting the ball. If they hit it, they can run. They *must* run on the third go, even if they don't hit the ball – unless the catcher catches the ball. If that happens, the batter is out.
- The batter runs to the bases in order. If they get around all four bases in one go, this is a home run.
- The batter can stop at any of the bases if they can't make a home run. They **remain** at the base until the next batter runs. Then they have to run on to the next base. Only one person is allowed on each base, so all the runners have to run on at the same time. Batters score a run when they get all the way back to home base without being out.
- When three batters are out, that is the end of the running team's innings (turn at batting).

How the game ends

Most rounders games have three, five or seven innings. The winning team is the one that has scored the most runs at the end of the *last* innings.

Did you know?

A good game of rounders **involves** lots of different skills. When you're batting and running, you need to **sprint** to the bases. You'll have to be fast if you want to score a home run! Rounders is also an **excellent** sport for developing hand–eye **coordination**. Batters need to watch the ball and swing the bat **accurately** to hit it. Catchers and fielders need to stay **alert** to catch the ball. Pitchers need to judge their throws carefully and make sure they are accurate. In a good rounders game, everyone improves their skills and everyone has fun!

A. Comprehension: Fact finding

Answer the questions.

1. List three places where the text says you can play rounders.
2. What do fielders have to do in a game of rounders?
3. What might you use squares of carpet or cardboard for?
4. Where on the pitch does the catcher stand?
5. What is a home run?

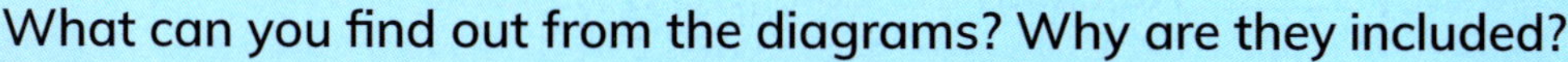

What can you find out from the diagrams? Why are they included?

B. Comprehension: Read between the lines

Answer the questions.

1. What kind of rounders match doesn't need a referee? Why?
2. Why do you think the author uses bullet points in the rules? What is unusual about the bullet points?
3. How might a friendly game of rounders be different from an official one?
4. Why is it important to have rules for a game like rounders?
5. Do you think these instructions are easy to follow? Why or why not?

Why are the distances given in 'strides'.

C. Vocabulary

Choose the word or phrase that is nearest in meaning to the underlined word.

1. Dana crossed the room in three long <u>strides</u>.
   a) hops **b)** minutes **c)** steps **d)** legs
2. I hope we get the <u>opportunity</u> to beat the other team!
   a) chance **b)** luck **c)** score **d)** ability
3. Make sure the fielders <u>remain</u> on the pitch.
   a) concentrate **b)** play **c)** stay **d)** stand
4. The batter suddenly started to <u>sprint</u> to first base.
   a) walk **b)** limp **c)** bat **d)** run
5. Although we lost the match, we had an <u>excellent</u> time!
   a) very good **b)** miserable **c)** boring **d)** pleasant
6. I went to <u>retrieve</u> the scarf I'd dropped.
   a) tidy **b)** fetch **c)** give away **d)** replace

Write three words or phrases that mean the opposite of 'excellent'.

D. Vocabulary

Choose the most suitable word to complete each sentence.

1. A ________ game can be played in different ways. (sporty, versatile, helpful)
2. The fielders ________ to get the batters out. (attempt, remain, repeat)
3. Can you tell me what the game ________? (attempts, supplies, involves)
4. Fielders need good hand–eye ________. (alert, coordination, training)
5. Use a ruler to measure more ________. (quickly, excellently, accurately)
6. You need to stay ________ to catch the ball. (alert, versatile, away)

Choose three answer words. Write sentences showing their meaning.

E. Grammar: Apostrophes of possession

Apostrophes of possession show that a thing belongs to someone or something.

Example: The dog's fur was covered in stinky mud.

When the owner is plural (more than one), put the apostrophe after the 's'.

Example: The players' jerseys were yellow and blue.

Put the apostrophes in the correct place to show possession.

1. Jack ate all of Laurens cake.
2. Both the boys phones were set to silent.
3. All the girls boots were muddy.
4. Many birds favourite food is worms.
5. Jakes book was torn.
6. The mouses ears were tiny and pink.

Add 's or s' to the underlined word in each sentence.

1. The <u>girl</u> lunchboxes were full of sandwiches and fruit.
2. We found the <u>dragon</u> treasure in its dark, rocky cave.
3. My <u>brother</u> bedrooms are both very untidy.
4. The tiny <u>kitten</u> fur was white and fluffy.
5. Through the trees, we saw the <u>witch</u> cottage.
6. All the football <u>player</u> jerseys were dirty.

Write three sentences about animals, using apostrophes to show possession.

F. Writing skills: Keeping things simple

Procedure texts such as rules and instructions need to be **simple and easy to understand**.

It is important to keep sentences short and not include **unnecessary information**.

These sentences are from *How to Play Rounders*, but unnecessary information has been added. Write the sentences correctly.

1. All batters get the opportunity to bat which is only fair.
2. The batter must try to hit the ball really, really, really hard to stop the catcher from catching it. It's not as easy as it sounds!
3. The batter can stop at first base, second base or third base if they can't make a home run or if they get too tired.

Write the instructions for Snakes and Ladders, leaving out unnecessary information.

Each player puts their counter on the space that says 'start here'. Everyone has their own favourite colour counter, like blue or red. Take it in turns to roll the dice. Don't roll them off the table! Move your counter forward the number of spaces shown on the dice, hopefully you get a big number like five or six. If your counter lands at the bottom of a ladder, you can move up to the top. That's the best! If your counter lands on the head of a snake, you must slide down to the bottom which is annoying since you can go all the way back to the start. The first player to get to the space that says 'home' is the winner.

G. Writing genre: Planning a procedure

Plan a procedure about how to play a game.

1. Think of a game that is fun but quick and easy to play. It could be:
   - ★ Hide and Seek
   - ★ Snakes and Ladders
   - ★ Stuck in the Mud
   - ★ Something else!
2. Make notes in your copy.
   - What equipment is needed?
   - Do players need to be in teams?
   - What do players/teams do?
   - How does the game end?

3. Think of section headings to help you organise your notes.

3b Hopping, Jumping Snacks

After intense exercise, your body needs to **recover**. It needs rest – and it also needs food and drink! Eating a healthy snack after exercise brings lots of **benefits**.

When you exercise hard, you use up lots of energy. Your body's energy needs replacing. Otherwise, you will end up feeling tired and **droopy**. A healthy snack will help **boost** your energy levels. Then you can tackle the rest of the day with **enthusiasm**!

Your muscles have to work hard during exercise. They need **protein** to help them recover and grow stronger. As your muscles' strength increases, you'll notice improvements. You'll find it easier to do sports and **energetic** activities.

Your body uses up a lot of liquid when you exercise – especially if you get hot and sweaty. You need to replace this by drinking plenty of **fluids**. Water is a good choice, and so is milk. Milk is also a good **source** of protein!

There are lots of protein- and carbohydrate-rich foods you could eat after exercise. But have you ever thought about eating insects? It may sound **bizarre**, but insects are actually a **superb** source of healthy protein. Did you know that crickets contain more protein than beef? What's more, eating crickets involves a lot less waste. However hard you try, you'll never eat a whole cow. But crickets' whole bodies are **edible**. They're surprisingly delicious, too. Don't believe me? Try the healthy biscuit recipe on the next page!

Oaty Cricket Crunchers

Ingredients:

50 g butter (at room temperature)
50 g caster sugar
1 tbsp honey
1 egg
80 g porridge oats
50 g dry-roasted crickets (chopped)
50 g wholemeal flour
1 tsp baking powder
1 tsp ground cinnamon or ginger (**optional**)

Equipment:

2 baking trays
Greaseproof paper
2 mixing bowls
Wooden spoon
Small bowl or mug
Fork
Oven gloves

Method

1. Ask an adult to preheat the oven to 200°C/gas mark 6. Line the baking trays with greaseproof paper.
2. Put the butter and sugar in one of the mixing bowls. Use the wooden spoon to beat them until they are soft and light. Then beat in the honey.
3. Break the egg into the small bowl or mug. Lightly **whisk** it with the fork.
4. Add the whisked egg to the bowl with the butter and sugar. Beat them all together.
5. In the other mixing bowl, mix the oats, crickets, flour, baking powder and spices (if you are using them).
6. Tip the dry mixture into the bowl with the butter mixture. Stir well to **combine** all the ingredients.

7. Drop tablespoons of the mixture onto the baking trays. Allow a few centimetres of space between spoonfuls. The biscuits will spread slightly in the oven.
8. Ask an adult to place the baking trays in the oven. Cook for 10–12 minutes. The biscuits are ready when they are a light golden colour.
9. Ask an adult to take the trays out of the oven. The biscuits will be slightly soft. Leave them on the trays for 2 minutes to harden a little.
10. Transfer the biscuits to the wire rack to cool completely.
11. Enjoy your biscuits with a glass of milk for extra protein!

Tip

If you're too **squeamish** to use crickets, don't worry! You can use raisins, nuts or chocolate chips instead.

Evaluate

How did you feel about eating crickets before you made the biscuits? Did you change your mind when you tasted them? Do you think these biscuits would encourage other people to try eating insects?

Did you know?

Cool cricket facts!

- Only male crickets chirp. They do this to attract a female.
- Male crickets make their chirping noise by rubbing their wings together.
- Crickets chirp at different rates depending on the temperature – the higher the temperature the higher the rate.
- A cricket's 'ears' are on its front legs.
- Cricket fighting is a popular pastime in China.

A. Comprehension: Fact finding

Answer the questions.

1. Apart from food, what does your body need after exercise?
2. Name two reasons why you should drink milk after exercise.
3. How much butter is used in the biscuit recipe?
4. What temperature should you set the oven to?
5. What is the small bowl or mug used for?

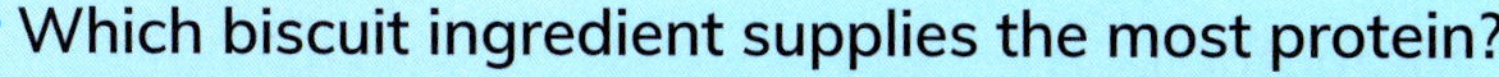

Which biscuit ingredient supplies the most protein?

B. Comprehension: Read between the lines

Answer the questions.

1. Why is it important to eat protein after exercise?
2. Give two reasons why people should eat crickets.
3. Why do you think the ingredients are listed in this order?
4. Why is it important to get an adult's help with the oven?
5. Why do you think the author chose the title for this text?

If you made these biscuits, would you add crickets? Explain your answer.

C. Vocabulary

Choose the word or phrase that is nearest in meaning to the underlined word.

1. After the race, it took my legs a long time to recover.
   a) feel better **b)** collapse **c)** exercise **d)** wobble
2. There are many benefits to keeping fit.
   a) pleasures **b)** upsides **c)** exceptions **d)** downsides
3. You can boost your fitness by taking regular exercise.
   a) destroy **b)** improve **c)** ignore **d)** support
4. If you think eating crickets is bizarre, try maggots!
   a) delicious **b)** wrong **c)** disgusting **d)** strange
5. The biscuits tasted superb.
   a) wonderful **b)** unpleasant **c)** strong **d)** mild
6. Use a wooden spoon to combine the ingredients.
   a) measure **b)** divide **c)** mix **d)** remove

Write dictionary definitions for two of the underlined words.

D. Vocabulary

Choose the most suitable word to complete each sentence.

energetic squeamish droopy whisk enthusiasm optional

1. Adding crickets to your biscuits is ______.
2. Some people feel ______ about eating insects.
3. I felt more ______ after my snack.
4. Before you add the egg, you have to ______ it.
5. Sean has lots of ______ for football.
6. I didn't have time to eat lunch, so I felt a bit ______.

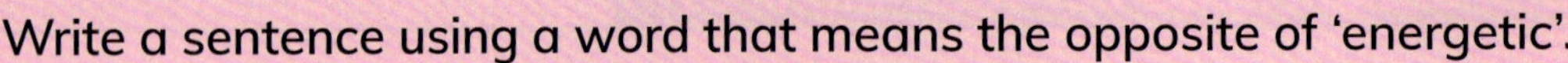

Write a sentence using a word that means the opposite of 'energetic'.

E. Grammar: Apostrophes of contraction

A **contraction** is a shortened form of two words. In contractions, we use an **apostrophe** in place of the missing letters.

Examples: they are → **they're** you have → **you've**

Write the sentences, changing the underlined words into contractions.

1. It is not time for school yet.
2. You are lucky Mr Connolly did not see you.
3. It is going to be a fun day out.
4. We are going to see a film that is about monsters.
5. I have never seen such a mess!
6. He will get in trouble if he does not tidy up.

Write the sentences using apostrophes for contractions.

1. Were doing a project on France, and its taking ages to finish.
2. Elaine and Mara say theyve finished already, but I think theyre lying.
3. Mam says that if were good well go ice-skating at the weekend.
4. Ive won the race but now Im all hot and sweaty.
5. Theres a lovely cake on the table, but unfortunately it isnt for us.
6. We couldnt go to Cork yesterday because the buses werent running.

Find three apostrophes of contraction in the text.

F. Writing skills: Instructions with bossy verbs

Verbs are doing, being or action words. Procedure texts, such as instructions, often use **bossy verbs** to tell the reader what to do.

Examples: Break the egg, **sift** the flour, **mix** the butter and sugar.

Look again at *Hopping, Jumping Snacks.*

1. Find three bossy verbs and write them down.
2. Add three more bossy verbs of your own to your list.

These instructions for how to make a sandwich have lost their bossy verbs. Read the text, then follow the instructions.

_______ two slices of bread.
_______ the bread slices with butter or mayonnaise.
_______ the filling on top of one slice of bread.
_______ the other slice of bread on top of the filling.

1. Choose bossy verbs to complete each step.
2. Write one more instruction to finish the text. Don't forget the bossy verb!

List some bossy verbs you could use to tell someone how to complete an obstacle course.

G. Writing genre: Writing a procedure

Use the notes you made in Unit 4a to write a procedure for how to play a game.

1. List the equipment needed. Use the heading 'What you need'.
2. Write the instructions in the order they happen in the game. Use the heading 'What to do'.
3. Remember to tell the reader how the game ends.
4. Don't forget to use bossy verbs!
5. Swap instructions with a partner. Can you follow each other's instructions? Is anything missing? Make suggestions for improvements.
6. Edit your instructions if you need to, using your partner's suggestions.

Your instructions could be part of a class book of favourite games!

4a Letting Go

'Come on, Tadhg, let go. You can do it!'

Tadhg **grasped** the wall as tightly as he could. His heart was pounding in his ears and his mouth was dry. He could hear Alesha encouraging him **earnestly** from the ground below, but her words were distant. She seemed to be a million miles away.

'It's gonna be fine, I promise. *Just let go!*'

He didn't know how long he had been up here, but it felt like hours. He was gripping the wall so hard his fingertips had turned white. He stared at them, too scared to look down. This whole thing felt like a **cruel** joke. Why did Alesha have to pick indoor climbing for her birthday party? Why couldn't she have just had a pizza party like every other kid in their class?

The instructor had arrived. Tadhg could hear Alesha telling him everything. It wouldn't be long before the other kids knew, and then the whole class would be laughing at him. His cheeks burned at the thought.

'Check your harness, Tadhg.' The instructor's calm voice floated up. 'Did you clip in like I showed you?'

Tadhg glanced at his harness. A large, metal clip connected him to a thick, black cord that ran up to the ceiling. He had **fumbled** a bit with the clip at first, but eventually got it hooked on. He nodded slowly.

'Good. You're attached to the **auto-belay**. Just let go and it will lower you gently back down to the ground. OK?'

Tadhg knew that already. He had watched Alesha do it before him. The way she had **faultlessly descended** from the wall made it seem so easy. It was easy for *her,* of course – she went climbing with her big sister every week. She was able to zip up the walls and sail **expertly** back down without even breaking a sweat.

'It's the most amazing feeling, Tadhg,' she had said, unclipping the cord from her harness. She handed it to him **casually**. 'You just let go and – *whoosh* – all the way back down! Want to have a go?' And even though his legs had felt **rooted** to the spot, he said yes. He wanted Alesha to think he was brave, daring – like she was.

Climbing up was fine. About halfway up, Tadhg even started to enjoy himself. All he had to do was keep moving his hands and feet from hold to hold, pressing the toes of his climbing shoes against the wall like the instructor had showed them. But then he reached the top … and made the terrible mistake of looking back down.

The drop was dizzying. Tadhg was so high up that Alesha and the other kids looked like ants. He couldn't just *let go.* What if the auto-belay broke? What if the clip was loose, or his harness snapped? He must have been a hundred metres high – no, *two* hundred. He'd be **flattened** like a dropped cake and they'd have to scrape him off the floor. So, he held on, even though he was sweaty and tired and his arms were aching. He didn't care what anyone said. He was *not* going to let go.

The instructor sighed impatiently.

'If you don't want to let go, just climb back down the same way you went up,' he said.

Tadhg swallowed hard. He lowered his right foot, feeling along the wall for the next hold. But his arms were trembling, and his palms were damp with sweat. Just as his foot found the hold, his right hand slipped off the wall. His left hand followed, and then his left foot, and suddenly he was falling, tumbling through the air … until, about a second later, his descent slowed. The auto-belay was working. Now he was sailing smoothly towards the ground, legs **dangling**, a light breeze **ruffling** his hair.

Tadhg's fear **vanished**. This was better than going down a slide, better than whizzing through the air on a tyre swing, better than the highest jump on a trampoline. He realised that he was laughing. He wanted the feeling to last forever, but moments later his feet gently touched the ground. Alesha was beside him in a flash. She threw her arms around Tadhg's shoulders and squeezed so hard it knocked the breath out of him.

'I was so worried!' she gasped. 'Are you OK?'

Tadhg nodded. He was better than OK. He was **exhilarated**. He found himself moving back towards the wall, putting his left foot up, then his left hand, his right foot …

'Tadhg?' Alesha called. 'What are you doing?'

Tadhg smiled. He looked up to the top of the wall where he had been only seconds ago.

'I'm going again,' he said.

Kerri Ward

A. Comprehension: Fact finding

Answer the questions.

1. What is Tadhg holding on to at the start of the story?
2. Who says, 'Just let go!'?
3. What sort of party would Tadhg have preferred to go to?
4. Why was Alesha already good at climbing?
5. What made Tadhg start to feel frightened?

What do you learn about Tadhg's character in this story?

B. Comprehension: Read between the lines

Answer the questions.

1. How does Tadhg feel about others laughing at him? How do you know?
2. Why do you think Tadhg tried climbing even though he was scared?
3. Do you think Tadhg was really in danger? Why or why not?
4. Why do you think the instructor 'sighed impatiently'?
5. Do you find the ending surprising? Why or why not?

In your opinion, who is the bravest character in the story? Why?

C. Vocabulary

Choose the word or phrase that is nearest in meaning to the underlined word.

1. I grasped the rail to stop myself from falling.
   a) leaped **b)** spotted **c)** hit **d)** grabbed
2. 'It's cruel to tease animals,' said Sophie.
   a) unkind **b)** understandable **c)** all right **d)** boring
3. Anne-Marie strolled casually through the park.
   a) in a relaxed way **b)** helplessly **c)** briskly **d)** slowly
4. Aiden skated faultlessly across the empty ice rink.
   a) clumsily **b)** perfectly **c)** helplessly **d)** innocently
5. The skier swished expertly down the slope.
   a) quickly **b)** cleverly **c)** skilfully **d)** helpfully
6. Tadhg's feet were rooted to the floor.
   a) near **b)** sunk **c)** falling **d)** stuck

Write three other words or phrases that have a similar meaning to 'cruel'.

D. Vocabulary

Choose the most suitable word to complete each sentence.

vanished fumbled ruffling earnestly descended exhilarated

1. Max almost caught the ball, but in the end he ______ it.
2. 'I didn't eat the last biscuit, really I didn't!' said Eoin ______.
3. Before I could catch up, Ella______ around the corner.
4. Tadhg's descent from the wall left him feeling ______.
5. We wearily ______ the mountain after reaching the summit.
6. The wind was ______ the leaves at the tops of the trees.

Write one new sentence using any two words from the box.

E. Grammar: Direct and indirect speech (part 1)

Direct speech gives the exact words someone says, using speech marks.
Example: 'You've got tomato sauce on your nose, Tom,' said Ellen.
Indirect speech tells roughly what someone says, without speech marks.
Example: Ellen told Tom that he had tomato sauce on his nose.

Write which sentences are direct speech and which are indirect speech.

1. 'How many times do I have to tell you?' asked Mam.
2. Dad complained that we had left the lights on again.
3. 'I can't believe you like worms,' said Ali.
4. Mrs Byrne told Jake to pick his coat up off the floor.
5. The garda shouted at us to stop.

Write the sentences as direct speech.

1. Mam said we should hurry up or we'd be late for school.
2. Mr Baxter told us we could eat our lunches after the match.
3. Arthur asked for a strawberry ice cream.

Write the sentences as indirect speech.

1. 'Keep off the grass!' the gardener told us.
2. 'Would you like to come to my party, Alice?' asked Carrie.
3. 'I'm cold,' said Nick.

Write what Tadhg might say to Alesha about his climb. Use direct speech.

F. Writing skills: Writing an effective story opening

An **effective story opening** grabs the reader's interest. It can do this with:

- Exciting action
- Powerful language
- Dialogue.

Example:

Tadhg grasped the wall as tightly as he could **(exciting action)**. His heart was pounding in his ears and his mouth was dry **(powerful language)**. 'Come on, Tadhg. You can do it!' **(dialogue)**.

Rewrite this story opening to be more effective. Include dialogue, action and powerful language.

Sam, Lucy and Dan were walking down the road when Lucy disappeared.

G. Writing genre: Planning a narrative

Narratives (stories) usually have **three Ps** – **Person**, **Place and Problem**. The problem is usually solved by the end of the story.

Study the story plan below for *The Wizard of Oz*.

Person
A young girl called Dorothy from Kansas

Place
Dorothy is magically transported to a place called 'Oz'.

Problem
Dorothy wants to get home, but she doesn't know how.

Plan a story about a person who has to be brave.

Choose a person, place and problem from the table below, or come up with ideas of your own. Create a plan for your story like the one shown above.

Person	Place	Problem
A 10-year-old boy	A school yard	Someone is being bullied
A knight	A faraway kingdom	A dragon is attacking the castle
An animal rescuer	A forest	A deer is caught in a trap

4b Keeping Pace

This story is set in Ethiopia. Solomon's grandfather has taken ill on a trip to the city. Solomon must get back to his home village quickly to find help. But the bus breaks down, and there won't be another until tomorrow. So Solomon has no choice. He'll have to run all the way home.

I know things now about running that I didn't know back then. That day, I learned the most important thing of all, and here's what it is. Running isn't all about your legs and arms. They do the work, of course (your legs especially), but what really matters is what's going on inside your head.

You have to get your mind into a place where it's not worrying about tiredness. It's not thinking about the soreness in your feet, or the ache in your legs, or the pain in your lungs.

I didn't know then how to **pace** myself and I started off much too fast. I sprinted down the road, away from the bus and all the **gawping** passengers, as if a lion was chasing me. I had to slow down in the end, of course, because I had a stitch in my side, and I was so puffed that I could hardly breathe. It was then that I began to think. Only it wasn't just me inside my head. Grandfather was there too.

'Calm down,' I could hear him saying. 'You haven't been stung by a bee, and there isn't actually a lion on your tail. Keep to the same pace. Nice and steady.'

Nice and steady. Nice and steady.
Nice and steady.

The words repeated themselves over and over again, making a **rhythm** for my legs to keep to. Then, when I'd settled into my pace, a number game took over.

First I counted my strides to the top of the next rise.

One, two, three, four …

And when I'd reached the top, I'd count myself down the **slope** to the bridge over the stream in the dip below.

… fifty-nine, sixty, sixty-one …

You can't keep counting forever, though. I got really bored and lost my **focus** after a while. That's when the worrying took over.

What if Grandfather doesn't make it? I thought. *I've left him on his own in Addis Ababa. What if the hospital doesn't take him in? I should have gone back with all those other people when the bus broke down. I was crazy to think I could run all this way. How far have I come so far, anyway?*

My legs started to feel heavy and my pace **faltered**. And then a truck came roaring up behind me, forcing me off the **tarmac** on to the edge of the road, where I was afraid my feet would get cut up by the sharp stones.

My chest started to **heave** with a sort of horrible panic. Then, just when I needed him, Grandfather came back into my head. He hadn't panicked. He'd jumped out of a truck on to the back of a horse and then he'd run for his life.

Nice and steady, Solomon, I heard him say. *Nice and steady.*

I found my rhythm again. I was running properly once more. I forced myself back to counting, not my paces, this time, but anything else I could see – the telegraph poles running alongside the road, then the birds sitting on the wires, and the farmhouses on the hillside, and the trees **edging** the bit of land round a church.

There wasn't much traffic luckily. Occasionally, a truck or a car came past. I easily overtook the farmers riding their donkeys, or children walking home from school. A few people called out greetings and questions to me, but mostly they left me alone. I was glad. I didn't want to waste my breath answering them.

I'd been going for what felt like hours and hours, on and on, up one hill and down the next, when I heard a **familiar** roaring noise behind me. I looked over my shoulder, and saw the bus! It was coming up fast. I waved at it **frantically**.

'Stop!' I yelled. 'It's me! I paid my fare!'

The driver didn't recognise me. He **blasted** his horn to get me out of the way, and raced past.

Extract from The Fastest Boy in the World *by Elizabeth Laird, published by Macmillan Children's Books, 2014.*

A. Comprehension: Fact finding

Answer the questions.

1. Why does Solomon have to run back to his village?
2. What mistake does Solomon make when he starts running?
3. What game does Solomon play to keep his mind occupied?
4. What town is Grandfather in?
5. Why is Solomon glad that few people try to speak to him?

How do you think Solomon felt when the bus didn't stop for him?

B. Comprehension: Read between the lines

Answer the questions.

1. Explain what Solomon learns about running in the story.
2. Does Solomon really hear his Grandfather's voice? Explain your answer.
3. Why has the author used italics for some words on pages 48 and 49?
4. Why does Solomon think it's lucky that there isn't much traffic?
5. Why do you think Solomon felt like he had been running for 'hours and hours'?

Do you think Solomon will be able to reach home? Explain your views.

C. Vocabulary

Choose the word or phrase that is nearest in meaning to the underlined word.

1. The children were <u>gawping</u> at the television.
   a) smiling **b)** staring **c)** scowling **d)** waving
2. I coasted down the <u>slope</u> on my skateboard.
   a) street **b)** hill **c)** side **d)** kerb
3. Danny's voice <u>faltered</u> when he realised we were listening.
   a) rose **b)** vanished **c)** got louder **d)** wobbled
4. There was a big puddle on the <u>tarmac</u>.
   a) field **b)** floor **c)** road surface **d)** horizon
5. The man waved <u>frantically</u>, hoping to attract our attention.
   a) desperately **b)** quickly **c)** lazily **d)** strangely
6. The car's horn <u>blasted</u> across the street.
   a) blared **b)** disappeared **c)** drifted **d)** was heard

Write dictionary definitions for two of the underlined words.

D. Vocabulary

Choose the most suitable words to complete the paragraph.

pace focus rhythm heave familiar

Janna gripped the oars and started rowing. At first she was slow and unsteady. 'Just ________,' Janna told herself. Gradually, her ________ increased and the ________ of her rowing became steadier. It was hard work, though, and her chest began to ________ with the effort of breathing. Soon, she was rowing fast. Just before crossing the finish line, she spotted the ________ faces of her family in the crowd, cheering her on.

Write two sentences about a sport, using at least two words from the box.

E. Grammar: Direct and indirect speech (part 2)

Remember: **direct speech** gives the exact words someone says, using speech marks. **Indirect speech** tells roughly what someone says, without speech marks.

Write the sentences, turning the direct speech into indirect speech.

1. 'I'm going into town,' said Dad. 'Do you want to come?'
   Dad said that he was going into town, and asked if we wanted to come.
2. 'I keep trying,' complained Ben, 'but I still can't skip.'
3. 'Have you all done your homework?' asked Mrs Keenan.
4. 'If you wait, James, you can have some cake, too,' promised Ciara.
5. 'Remember to brush your teeth,' the dentist told us.
6. 'Go away, Declan!' snapped Amber.

Write the text, turning the indirect speech into direct speech. Start a new line each time there is a new speaker.

Mam asked Aoife to set the table for supper. Aoife told Mam that she'd come and do it in a minute. Mam got cross, and asked Aoife to come and do it at once. Then Aoife sulkily said that she was coming. When Aoife smelled spaghetti Bolognese, she cheered up. She told Mam that was her very favourite dinner!

Write the last conversation you had. Use either direct or indirect speech.

F. Writing skills: Writing action

The **action** in a story is what happens in the plot. Writers often try to make the action more exciting by using powerful language, dialogue and details.

Example: Nadia leaped into the air, higher than she had ever jumped before. As she vaulted over the high jump bar, she heard Ms Mulligan's voice in the crowd, urging her on. 'You can do it, Nadia – I know you can!'

Improve the story opening below.

- Replace some of the verbs with more interesting ones.
- Add some dialogue.
- Try to include some extra detail.

Jake was swimming. He knew that Carlo was right behind him. He didn't want to let Carlo catch him. Jake went fast, but Carlo was going even faster.

Look at the picture. Write the first paragraph of a story about it, using powerful verbs and some dialogue. Can you include some interesting details?

G. Writing genre: Writing a narrative

Use the plan you made in Unit 4a to write a story.

1. When writing the action in your story, make sure you include:
   - Some exciting events
   - How the characters feel
   - Some powerful verbs
   - What they do and say.
2. Read your story out loud to your partner and ask for feedback.
   - Was the story exciting? Did it all make sense?
   - Was your problem solved by the end of the story?
3. Write the final draft of your story, making any improvements you can.

5a Film Magic: How Do Movie Special Effects Work?

Think of your favourite film. The funniest or most exciting parts may have been created using special effects. Film-makers want us to believe in magic, fantasy creatures and **gigantic** explosions. But have you ever wondered just how special effects work? How do they trick us into believing the impossible?

There are lots of different kinds of special effects. Here are just some of them explained!

Computer generated effects

Computer effects are used in lots of films today. It takes a large team of **animators** many months to create an animated movie. They start by making digital models of the characters and settings. Complicated mathematical **calculations** are used to work out how the characters move. It takes a lot of **complex** programming to make this look lifelike! If an animation gets this wrong, it doesn't look good at all. Things like hair and clothing are particularly tricky to make **realistic**.

Some films use **motion capture** as well as **computer generated effects**. In motion capture, first you film an actor moving in real life. Then you transfer those movements to the computer to create an animation. The character of Gollum in *The Lord of the Rings* films was made with motion capture.

Did you know?

Animators have to model 400,000 separate hairs on each character's head and animate them so that every hair moves in a realistic way!

Actor Andy Serkis and his character in *The Lord of the Rings*, Gollum

Optical illusions

Sometimes amazing effects can be made without computer animation! You've probably wondered how Hagrid in the *Harry Potter* films looks so large. In fact, two actors played Hagrid. The main one was Robbie Coltrane, who's just 1.8 m tall. An actor 2 m tall was also used for some scenes. This made Hagrid look even bigger! There were also two versions of Hagrid's hut. A larger version of the hut made other characters, like Harry and Hermione, look small. And a smaller version was used to make Hagrid look enormous!

Make-up

Special make-up can completely change an actor's **appearance**. Make-up artists spend many hours creating **moulds**. They're designed to fit over the actor's face or body to make them look different.

The child actor, Jacob Tremblay, played Auggie in the film *Wonder*. He had to spend one and a half hours every day getting ready! The make-up designer created a special **artificial** head for the character. Jacob had to wear it like a sort of helmet.

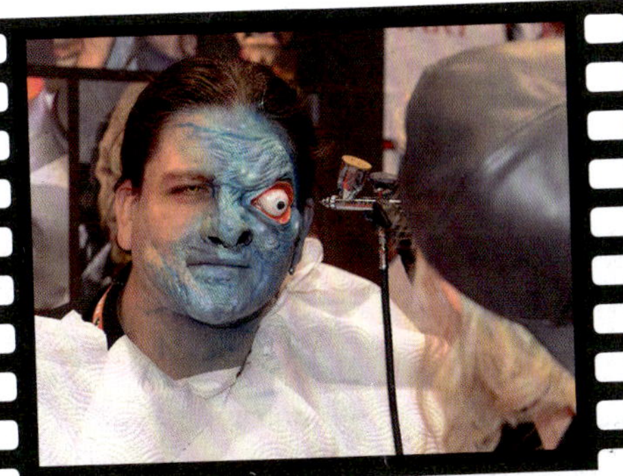

Jacob Tremblay as Auggie in Wonder

Animatronics

Animatronics are a bit like puppets. They're extremely **realistic** moving models that can be enormous or tiny. One of the largest animatronics ever made was a Tyrannosaurus rex. This monster starred in the 1993 movie *Jurassic Park*. It was made with a metal skeleton **encased** in foam rubber skin. The enormous model was over 6 m tall and over 12 m long! It took 12 people to move it. The model amazed the film's audience. It helped to win the film three Oscars.

Miniatures

The film *King Kong* was made in the 1930s. Ever since then, film-makers have used **miniature** models to create amazing illusions. When *King Kong* was made there were no computer special effects. The film-makers wanted to show a huge ape **towering** over New York. So they had to create a tiny model city and a big model ape! Nowadays, the effects in *King Kong* don't look that realistic. However, this illusion amazed audiences back in the 1930s.

Modern films can use computer generated effects to show this type of scene. But film-makers still often use models too. For example, this castle in the *Harry Potter* films is a small-scale model!

Conclusion

Now you know how some film special effects are created. Next time you watch a film, look out for some of these **techniques**. But don't think about it too much in case it spoils the magic of the film!

A. Comprehension: Fact finding

Answer the questions.

1. How do animators work out how characters should move?
2. Name a film character created using motion capture.
3. Name **two** ways Hagrid was made to look so big.
4. What film part did Jacob Tremblay play?
5. What was the animatronic dinosaur in *Jurassic Park* made of?

Would you like to work in movie special effects? Why or why not?

B. Comprehension: Read between the lines

Answer the questions.

1. Why do you think it takes so long to make an animated movie?
2. Name one upside and one downside to using moulded make-up.
3. How do the pictures in this unit help you understand the text?
4. Why did the T-Rex animatronic need to be so big?
5. Which of the special effects listed do you think is hardest to create?

Why do you think special make-up is still used, as well as computer effects?

C. Vocabulary

Choose the word that is nearest in meaning to the underlined word.

1. Jamie gasped when he saw the <u>gigantic</u> spider.
   a) hungry **b)** huge **c)** scary **d)** friendly
2. The maths homework Mrs Whelan set us is quite <u>complex</u>.
   a) easy **b)** boring **c)** long **d)** complicated
3. Computer animation makes impossible things look <u>realistic</u>.
   a) pleasant **b)** difficult **c)** lifelike **d)** ordinary
4. Actors use make-up and costumes to change their <u>appearance</u>.
   a) look **b)** character **c)** job **d)** opinion
5. The strawberries we bought were <u>encased</u> in plastic.
   a) wrapped **b)** stuck **c)** hidden **d)** delivered
6. The <u>miniature</u> model space ship was very detailed.
   a) animatronic **b)** tiny **c)** large **d)** moving

Write a sentence about a film or TV show, using 'realistic' or 'complex'.

D. Vocabulary

Choose the most suitable word to complete each sentence.

calculations   animators   artificial   techniques   moulds   towering

1. ______ make digital models of film characters and settings.
2. The huge animatronic dinosaur was ______ over the actors.
3. By my ______, the experiment should have worked.
4. The plant was ______, but it looked real.
5. Special make-up can be made using ______.
6. Model making and animation are two ______ used in films.

Choose two of the words in the box and use them in a sentence about films.

E. Grammar: 'a', 'an' and 'the'

Articles are used with nouns. They tell us whether a specific or general noun is being described.

The is the **definite article**. It describes specific nouns.

Examples: the Tyrannosaurus rex, **the** film *King Kong*.

A and **an** are **indefinite articles**. They describe general nouns. 'A' is used before nouns starting with a consonant. 'An' is used before nouns starting with a vowel.

Examples: a make-up artist, **an** actor.

Complete the sentences using 'a', 'an' or 'the'.

1. Would you like ____ banana or ____ orange?
2. ____ school will close at 1 p.m. today.
3. ____ doctor gave me ____ lollipop after my injection.
4. Sam has ____ sister but Jim is ____ only child.

Complete the passage using 'a', 'an' or 'the'.

One of ____ first movies ever made was called *Arrival of a Train*. It was ____ 50-second clip of ____ steam train, filmed in ____ French town of La Ciotat. There's ____ urban legend that ____ audience was so scared by the sight of ____ enormous train coming towards them, that they screamed and ran out of ____ room!

Write a sentence using 'a', 'an' and 'the'.

F. Writing skills: Subheadings

Explanation texts often contain **subheadings**.
Subheadings break information into clear sections.

Make a list of the subheadings in *Film Magic*.

Read these short sections from an explanation text about magic. Then write a subheading for each section.

Good magicians spend a lot of time practising! A lot of magic tricks are based on simple illusions. Although they are simple, it takes a lot of practice to make them look effective. If the magician hasn't practised enough, the audience will easily see through the trick.

One important skill for a magician is distraction. Magicians need to make sure the audience doesn't notice when they slip a playing card into their pocket. So they do or say something to distract the audience's attention at the key moment.

In the section 'Computer generated effects' on page 54, can you see a place where another subheading could be added? Write the extra subheading.

G. Writing genre: Planning an explanation

Plan an explanation text about a job in the film industry.

1. Choose one of the jobs listed above, then make a KWL chart.
2. Write what you already know about the job in the **K** column.
3. Write all the things you want to know in the **W** column.
4. Use books and the internet to research the answers to your questions. Write the answers in the **L** column.
5. Group your information under subheadings, such as:
   - Why the job is important
   - What the job involves
   - What skills are needed for the job
   - How this job helps to make a brilliant film.

5b What Do Stunt Performers Do?

Jumping out of burning buildings. Fighting terrifying monsters. Escaping in a high-speed car chase. Action movies are full of danger and excitement! Next time you're watching an exciting action **sequence**, think about the people who make it possible. These are the **stunt** performers.

Many famous actors like to do their own stunts. But sometimes the stunts are just too dangerous. You need to have special training to perform them safely. Sometimes a stunt requires a special skill that the actor doesn't have, like a **martial art**. That's where stunt performers come in! They stand in for the main actor when **risky** stunts are needed.

No two days are alike for a stunt performer. One day, they might be jumping from a high cliff into the sea. Maybe the next day, they're fighting a dragon on horseback. The day after that, they might be set on fire! It takes **exceptional** skills to do all these things safely and **convincingly**. So what's involved in being a stunt performer?

Training

People who want to become stunt performers in Ireland usually join either Stunt Register Ireland or Stunt Guild Ireland. Stunt Guild Ireland provides training so stunt performers can get special **qualifications**. It takes a long time to qualify. You've got to spend three years as a trainee stunt performer first. This means working on films with an experienced performer. They advise you and make sure you're safe. Then you spend another two years as a qualified stunt performer, working by yourself. After that, you can become a stunt coordinator. A stunt coordinator arranges stunts for other performers.

To qualify as a stunt performer, you'll need to be good at many different things. Most performers have a black belt in a martial art, such as judo or karate. You might train as a stunt driver, or qualify as a stunt motorcyclist or horse rider. You'll also need to learn how to climb – and how to fall! Many stunt performers have special qualifications. These could be in diving, parachuting, rock climbing or gymnastics.

Case study: Tristan McConnell

Stunt performer, Tristan McConnell, says: 'I'm a member of Stunt Register Ireland. There's a bunch of different skill-sets and qualifications that you must have to join. As a teenager, I was into sports and martial arts. I trained up to black belt in tae kwon do and was obsessed with rock climbing, so I had a head start. For my **additional** skills, I chose to do **specialised** training in horse riding and in swimming.'

Case study: Eimear O'Grady

Eimear O'Grady is a stunt coordinator and performer. She's performed in many films and TV shows. Working on a film often means a very early start. So Eimear may get to the studio at 6 a.m. Her working day might involve many different kinds of stunts. Sometimes, she stands in for an actor in a fight scene. She has to dress exactly like the actor. Then it looks as if the actor is doing the stunt.

Eimear's first big stunt was a 'car knockdown'. It had to look like a car had run her over. The car came up behind her and she had to **somersault** backwards over the top of it. Then she had to fall down behind the car. Eimear says, 'I was wearing a harness, which helped with the somersault. I didn't feel any pain. I had worked out my steps, so I knew what foot I was going to land on. That's the sort of attention to detail involved. I was very nervous the night before, but on the day, calmness descends on you. It's going to happen, you're going to do it, and you just do it.'

Making dangerous things safe

Stunt performers do a lot of risky things. But they always make sure to stay as safe as possible. They train hard and **acquire** lots of skills. They pay attention to the small details. They work hard to make stunts **believable** and exciting to watch!

A. Comprehension: Fact finding

Answer the questions.

1. Name **two** kinds of stunts mentioned in the text.
2. How long must you spend as a trainee stunt performer?
3. What do stunt coordinators do?
4. Which martial art is Tristan McConnell an expert in?
5. Why does Eimear O'Grady dress like the actor she is standing in for?

Why do stunt performers have to pay attention to details?

B. Comprehension: Read between the lines

Answer the questions.

1. Give **two** reasons why famous actors don't always do stunts.
2. Why do you think stunt performers need to train for so long?
3. Why is it important for stunt performers to know how to fall?
4. Name **two** ways Eimear stayed safe in the 'car knockdown'.
5. Would you like to be a stunt performer? Why or why not?

What kind of personality do you think a stunt performer needs to have?

C. Vocabulary

Choose the word or phrase that is nearest in meaning to the underlined word.

1. Eimear knew the car stunt was <u>risky</u>.
   a) difficult **b)** scary **c)** dangerous **d)** impossible
2. Stunt performers need to have <u>exceptional</u> fitness.
   a) extremely good **b)** unrealistic **c)** rare **d)** average
3. Erin played the part of the Ice Queen very <u>convincingly</u>.
   a) cleverly **b)** bravely **c)** believably **d)** helpfully
4. It was a hot day so we took <u>additional</u> bottles of water.
   a) large **b)** disposable **c)** full **d)** extra
5. The stunt looked very <u>believable</u> on screen.
   a) fake **b)** absurd **c)** realistic **d)** dangerous
6. Harry practised hard to <u>acquire</u> better football skills.
   a) find **b)** gain **c)** buy **d)** copy

Write sentences using 'exceptional' and 'risky'.

D. Vocabulary

Choose the most suitable words to complete the paragraph.

stunt somersault sequence qualifications specialised martial art

An expert _______ performer needs to train for over three years to gain their _______. It takes many highly _______ skills to perform a stunning _______ of stunts! Many stunt performers are skilled in a _______, and they may also be able to perform gymnastic moves such as a back flip or a _______.

Write dictionary definitions for two of the words from the box.

E. Grammar: Homophones

Homophones are words that sound the same but have different spellings and meanings.

Examples:

to	preposition showing direction
two	number
too	as well

their	belonging to them
they're	contraction of 'they are'
there	opposite of 'here'

Write the sentences using 'to', 'too' or 'two'.

1. We're going _____ the park. Would you like to come _____?
2. I ate _____ sandwiches, so I was _____ full for ice cream.
3. There were _____ people in the queue so I had _____ wait my turn.

Write the sentences using 'their', 'there' or 'they're'.

1. _____ all going to France tomorrow.
2. My bag is over _____ by the door.
3. Have you seen _____ cute new puppy?

Choose the correct homophone to complete each sentence.

1. To make a cake, you need _____, eggs, butter and sugar. (flour/flower)
2. We took a ferry across the Irish _____. (see/sea)
3. I had to _____ for the pizza to cook. (weight/wait)

Think of four more homophone pairs. List them in your copy.

F. Writing skills: Topic sentences and supporting details

In explanation texts, paragraphs sometimes begin with a **topic sentence**. This is a sentence that introduces the main idea.
This is usually followed by sentences containing **supporting details**.

Example:

Topic sentence: No two days are alike for a stunt performer.
Supporting details: One day, they might be jumping from a high cliff into the sea. Maybe the next day, they're fighting a dragon on horseback.

Look again at the text.

1. Find another paragraph that starts with a topic sentence. Write it down.
2. Find a sentence in the same paragraph that gives a supporting detail. Write it down.

Write a short paragraph on why being a stunt performer would be a fun job. Include:

- A topic sentence
- Three supporting details.

G. Writing genre: Writing an explanation

Use the KWL chart you made in Unit 5a to write an explanation about a job in the film industry.

1. Write your first draft. Remember to:
   - Give your explanation a title.
   - Use your subheadings to group your information.
   - Make sure that your paragraphs have topic sentences and supporting details.
   - Finish with a conclusion.
2. Check that your work is clearly organised. Write a second draft, making any improvements you can.

6a A Hobby for Everyone

St Patrick's National School Newsletter

Are you looking for a new challenge? Perhaps you want something to keep you **engrossed** through the long winter evenings? Below, three children from 4th Class tell us about their fantastic hobbies. Read on to find out why YOU should take up manga drawing, Irish dancing or bass guitar. You won't believe how much fun you could have!

Magnificent Manga

by Martha Baker

Do you enjoy drawing?

Do you like cute animals, complex characters and magical creatures?

Do you want to get **absorbed** in your own imaginary world?

If you've answered yes to any of these questions, manga drawing could be for you! Manga is a typically Japanese way of drawing comics and graphic novels. It's extremely cool!

I first became interested in manga because of my older brother, Peter. He had lots of manga books, and one day he lent me one. I was **overwhelmed** by the beauty of the pictures!

I **longed** to create something like this for myself. So I started practising! At first, my drawings weren't all that good.

But I **persevered**. Before long, I was able to draw pictures like the one on the right.

Drawing manga has brought me a lot of fun and **satisfaction**. It's wonderful to see the stories I imagine coming to life on paper! So why not join me? All you need is a pen and some paper – and you could create a whole new fantasy world of your own!

Dance Yourself Fit!

by Declan Boyle

When I took up Irish dancing two years ago, some of my friends were **incredulous**! They couldn't believe I was **willingly** signing up for dance classes. 'Aren't they just for girls?' they said. 'Are you going to get one of those sparkly dresses, Declan?' But now I've won a top prize at our local feis, they've changed their tune! One or two of them are even thinking of joining me.

So why should you take up Irish dancing – especially if you're a boy?

Well, the first reason is – it's fun! Anyone who loves Irish traditional music knows just how enjoyable it is to dance to. Why should girls have all the fun?

Secondly, if you're competitive, there are loads of Irish dancing competitions you can take part in. These are a great way to improve and can be really exciting too. I competed in three competitions last year and I even won a medal in one of them!

But the third reason is the one that means the most to me personally. Irish dancing is a fantastic way to keep fit! You need lots of endurance to keep up with the frantic pace of some dances. You need strong muscles too. And the **stamina** and strength you build up doing dance comes in very handy for other sports. I've improved at both football and running since I took up Irish dancing.

Don't believe me? Come along to my dance class next Wednesday and try it for yourself. You'll soon be hooked!

Why Learn Bass Guitar?

by Selina Murphy

Lots of people start off with a regular guitar as their first instrument. But if you love pop and rock, you should seriously **consider** learning the bass! I took it up back in the summer, when my cousin gave me his old bass as a birthday present. I've never looked back!

So what makes the bass guitar such a fantastic instrument? Here are just a couple of reasons.

It doesn't take long to learn. Although you need strong fingers to play on the bass's thick strings, it's quick to pick up the basics. After just a few lessons, you'll know enough to jam along to your favourite tracks. And not long after that, you could even start playing in a band!

A good bass guitar is a really important element of any pop or rock band's sound. The bass provides a strong rhythm and helps any band sound **professional** and cool. So if you're good, you'll definitely be in demand! Who knows – you could even be a rock star one day!

The bass guitar is fun, cool and not too difficult to play. What more could you want?

A. Comprehension: Fact finding

Answer the questions.

1. Who are the three children writing about their hobbies?
2. Which country does manga originally come from?
3. What other sports does Declan Boyle do?
4. What prompted Selina Murphy to start learning bass guitar?
5. Why do you need strong fingers to play the bass guitar?

Which of the three pieces do you find most persuasive? Why?

B. Comprehension: Read between the lines

Answer the questions.

1. Which hobby would appeal most to someone athletic? Why?
2. Which hobby would appeal most to someone shy? Why?
3. Why might bass guitar be a good hobby if you are impatient?
4. Which two hobbies might help you make new friends? Why?
5. Describe the personality of one of the three writers.

List one possible downside of each hobby.

C. Vocabulary

Choose the word or phrase that is nearest in meaning to the underlined word or phrase.

1. Adil was completely <u>absorbed in</u> the game.
   a) bored by **b)** distracted from **c)** included in **d)** occupied by
2. When she saw her presents, Diana was <u>overwhelmed</u>.
   a) stunned **b)** annoyed **c)** upset **d)** happy
3. Seamus <u>longed</u> for a puppy of his own.
   a) asked **b)** saved up **c)** wished **d)** worked
4. Gran was <u>incredulous</u> when she heard the news.
   a) disbelieving **b)** furious **c)** appalled **d)** happy
5. Maria showed lots of <u>stamina</u> on the pitch.
   a) ability **b)** energy **c)** courage **d)** intelligence
6. Patrick said he'd <u>consider</u> joining the football team.
   a) give up on **b)** think about **c)** forget about **d)** organise

Write a sentence about something you enjoy, using 'absorbed'.

D. Vocabulary

Choose the most suitable words to complete the paragraph.

engrossed satisfaction demand professional persevered willingly

I love making and painting model animals – it gives me a lot of _______ ! I'd _______ spend hours creating a complex model. Sometimes I stay _______ in what I'm doing for a whole morning! My finished models look very _______ . They're always in _______ from friends, who ask me to create models specially for them. I wasn't very good at model making to start with, but I _______ , and now it's my favourite thing to do in my spare time!

Write two words that have a similar meaning to 'satisfaction'.

E. Grammar: Nouns (part 1)

Nouns are naming words.

Common nouns are the general names for people, places, animals or things.

Examples: planet, girl, dog, county.

Proper nouns are the specific names of people, places, animals or things. Proper nouns always start with a capital letter.

Examples: Earth, Niamh, Tibbles, Dublin.

List the nouns and write 'common' or 'proper' next to each one.

1. Marie
2. Portugal
3. duck
4. author
5. newspaper
6. football
7. J.K. Rowling
8. Labrador

Write the sentences. Circle the common nouns and underline the proper nouns.

1. Isabel took a train across Europe to Poland.
2. My friend has a Shar Pei called Snuffles.
3. Jamie and Martha went to the cinema in Galway.
4. Mr O'Brien took us to Kilkenny Castle in the minibus.
5. Eve has an apple, a pen and a scarf in her bag.
6. Rabbits live in the fields near our house.

Write a sentence about yourself, using one proper noun and one common noun.

F. Writing skills: Know your audience

The **audience** is the person or people a text is written for. Thinking about **who** your audience is before writing a persuasive text can help you decide **how** to persuade them.

Example: Advertisement for a toy.

- **Who** is the audience? Children and their parents.
- **How** does the advertisement persuade them? By making the toy sound fun and good value.

Reread *A Hobby for Everyone* and choose the section that you find most persuasive.

1. Write **who** the audience for the text is.
2. Give examples of **how** the writer persuades the reader.

Read this short advert. Write **who** the audience is and **how** the author persuades them.

Get swimming!

Do you want to keep fit, have fun and make new friends your age? Come along to St Patrick's Over 60s Swimming Club! We meet every Thursday at 7 p.m. at the swimming pool on Connacht Lane. Everyone is welcome, from beginners to experts. Come and join our friendly club – you'll have a splashing time!

G. Writing genre: Planning a persuasive text

Plan a persuasive text to convince your friends to take up a hobby.

1. Choose a hobby. It could be something you do, or something you would like to do.
2. Write a list like this one:

Hobby:	Judo
Audience:	Other 4th Class children
Reasons to do it:	Judo is fun and exciting
	keeps you fit
	helps you make friends
	teaches you to respect others

3. How will you make it sound fun? Think of exciting words and phrases to persuade your audience to take up the hobby. Add your ideas to your list.

Come to the Purple Unicorn Festival!

How much fun can you handle? Are you ready for the Purple Unicorn Festival?

Ireland's top new family-friendly festival experience!

- Spend a summer weekend **luxuriating** in the lush green countryside.
- Relax and unwind to the latest tunes from world-class musicians.
- Set your children's imaginations free! With craft activities, sports, drama and music, there's truly something for everyone to enjoy.
- Enjoy a fabulous feast as you take your pick from the best of the world's **cuisines**.
- Camp in our beautiful woodland. You'll be **snug** in one of our top-of-the-range **yurts** or **tepees**.

Here's a taste of this year's festival highlights!

Music

Chart-topping band Sunset Revolt get the party started on Friday evening. Get set for a high-energy dance experience the whole family can enjoy!

On Saturday, get hands-on with African drums. Then swing and **sway** to the salsa beat. Old favourites Girlzone head the line-up for Saturday night.

On Sunday, chill out with the smooth sounds of Surf's Up. The festival comes to a **mellow** end with top folk duo, Sad Cypress.

Food

Set your tastebuds **tingling** with a walk down our Street Food Alley. We've got Southern US barbecues and burgers. We've got Asian noodles. We've got classic Italian pizzas from our wood-fired pizza ovens. Don't miss the Japanese sushi or Mexican tacos! Or for a **nostalgic** taste of home, we've also got good old fish and chips!

Children's activities

Get your children's weekend off to a **spectacular** start! There's a firelight singalong and fireworks on Friday night. Their feet won't touch the ground on Saturday as they **whisk** from one activity to another. They can try their hand at costume-making or pottery in the craft tent. They'll love our outdoor climbing wall and adventure playground! Creative types can put on a performance, with singing, dancing and laughter. And if they've still got energy to spare, never fear! You can tire them out with a range of sports and activities. Football, archery, abseiling, badminton – you name it, they'll get a chance to try it!

Don't delay – sign up today!

Just click this link to sign up for our email newsletter. We'll alert you as soon as tickets become available. You'll kick yourself if you miss it!

Purple Unicorn or Lame Donkey?

Festival review by Anna Jacobs (10) and Finn Jacobs (8)

We were really excited when Mam and Dad said we were going to the Purple Unicorn Festival. The **brochure** looked great! We could hardly wait to go camping in a tepee. All the fun activities sounded brilliant. Unfortunately, though, the promises made in the brochure didn't quite reflect reality.

Things got off to a bad start on the Friday evening. We went to the singalong, but the songs were really babyish. Worse still, there weren't any fireworks – just a couple of damp sparklers. We decided to have an early night. We booked a tent because the yurts and tepees were so expensive. But it was ripped and our spot was in a thistly field. We woke up in the middle of the night with prickles poking through our sleeping bags. NOT fun!

On Saturday morning we woke to a steady downpour of rain. Everything in our tent was soaked through! Mam and Dad were a bit grumpy by this stage. We decided to go and see what was happening in the craft tent. The answer was – not a lot. It was only 10 a.m. but they had already run out of clay for the pottery. Most of the outdoor activities were cancelled because of the rain. We did manage to have a fun kickaround with some other children, though.

The headline act for Saturday night, Girlzone, never showed up. Perhaps someone had told them how bad the food was! We had pizza for dinner – well, I think it was meant to be pizza. It was more like a wodge of soggy cardboard!

We had tickets for all three days of the festival. But we were glad when Mam and Dad decided to go home early. Will we be coming back next year? I don't think so!

A. Comprehension: Fact finding

Answer the questions.

1. How long does the Purple Unicorn Festival last?
2. Where do people sleep if they go to the festival?
3. Name three different types of food at the festival.
4. What are the ages of the children who wrote the review?
5. What did the children have for dinner, and what was it like?

Which was most persuasive – the festival brochure or the review? Why?

B. Comprehension: Read between the lines

Answer the questions.

1. Which festival activity would you like best? Why?
2. Who is the festival aimed at? How do you know?
3. Is the brochure from a newspaper or website? How do you know?
4. How did Anna and Finn's feelings about the festival change?
5. Did the children pick a good review title? Explain your answer.

Would you like to attend the Purple Unicorn Festival? Give reasons for your answer.

C. Vocabulary

Choose the word or phrase that is nearest in meaning to the underlined word.

1. I like Italian <u>cuisine</u>, especially pizza.
   a) cities **b)** restaurants **c)** cooking **d)** snacks
2. It was cold outside, but it was <u>snug</u> in the caravan.
   a) crowded **b)** cosy **c)** boiling hot **d)** uncomfortable
3. We were excited to sleep in a <u>tepee</u>.
   a) tent **b)** caravan **c)** cottage **d)** hammock
4. The music started playing and the dancers started to <u>sway</u>.
   a) jump **b)** fall **c)** move from side to side **d)** run
5. The campsite was in a <u>spectacular</u> forest setting.
   a) hidden **b)** difficult **c)** high up **d)** breathtaking
6. The <u>brochure</u> made the cycling holiday sound exciting.
   a) advertising booklet **b)** article **c)** review **d)** letter

Write dictionary definitions for two of the underlined words.

D. Vocabulary

Choose the most suitable word to complete each sentence.

1. At the campsite, everyone felt relaxed and ______ . (mellow, lush, sway)
2. The kitten lay by the fire, ______ in the warmth. (luxuriating, tingling, shivering)
3. ______ are big circular tents. (brochures, yurts, snugs)
4. My tastebuds started ______ at the thought of the delicious food. (luxuriating, swaying, tingling)
5. Dad felt ______ about his childhood. (snug, nostalgic, tingling)
6. A taxi arrived to ______ us quickly back home. (sway, whisk, lush)

Write a short paragraph using 'mellow', 'cosy' and 'snug'.

E. Grammar: Nouns (part 2)

Remember: **nouns** are naming words.

Common nouns are the general names of people, animals, places or things.

Proper nouns are the specific names of people, animals, places or things. Proper nouns always start with a capital letter.

Write the sentences, filling the gaps with common nouns.

1. I've always wanted a pet ______ , but a ______ would be fun too.
2. It was cold out, so Tom put on his ______ , ______ and ______ .
3. My favourite toy is my ______ , but Tadhg prefers his ______ .
4. For my birthday dinner, I had ______ , ______ and ______ .
5. I was amazed to see a huge ______ coming towards me across the ______ .
6. Ethan kindly let me borrow me his ______ .

Find all the proper nouns in this text. Write them in your copy.

It was a Saturday in November, and we were packing our suitcases for our trip to Poland. We were flying from Dublin Airport the next day. 'Don't forget to pack your gloves!' Mam told my sister, Julia.

'I can't find them!' Julia shouted. 'I must have dropped them in the Phoenix Park last week.' Just then, Auntie Marta arrived to pick up our pet pug, Rocky. Auntie Marta started to laugh. Julia's gloves were in Rocky's bed!

Write three proper and three common nouns from *Festival Fun?*

F. Writing skills: Persuasive language

Persuasive texts appeal to the reader in different ways.

- **Questions** draw the reader in.
  Example: How much fun can you handle?
- **Exclamations** make things sound exciting.
  Example: They'll love our outdoor climbing wall!
- **Commands** tell the reader to do something.
  Example: Sign up today!

Find and write a question, an exclamation and a command in this advert.

Are you tired and stressed? Do you need to relax?
Daily life can be exhausting. But never fear – the answer is here! Take up the relaxing hobby of knitting. You'll never look back! Join our knitting club and knowledgeable experts will help you perfect your skills.

Reread *Festival Fun?* Find and write the following.

- A question
- An exclamation
- A command.

G. Writing genre: Writing a persuasive text

Use the notes you made in Unit 6a to write a persuasive text convincing your friends to take up a new hobby.

1. Write your first draft. Remember to:
   - Think about who your audience is and how you will persuade them.
   - Use questions, exclamations and commands to draw the reader in and make them want to do what you say!
   - Use interesting words that will help readers imagine how great your hobby is!
2. Swap drafts with a partner and ask for feedback. Were they persuaded to try your hobby?
3. Edit your text to make it even more persuasive. Then write the final draft.

7a On the Trail of Ded Moroz

It was Christmas Eve in Dublin, but Detective Elvis O'Shaughnessy wasn't at home stuffing the turkey. He was working – heading up a new crime unit called Police Against **Supernatural** Threats and Aliens. Or PASTA for short. They'd been set up to **investigate** sightings of **mysterious** creatures like Martians, banshees and yetis and although they'd been in **operation** for almost a year, they'd not seen a single one. Every day Elvis worked late, hoping his wish would come true.

He was about to head home when one of his secret agents phoned from Russia.

'This is Spaghetti, PASTA, do you read me?'

Elvis shook his head. When he'd set up the special crime unit all his secret agents had **insisted** on having silly pasta code-names. Why couldn't they have chosen normal secret agent names like Red Fox or Delta Seven?

'Loud and clear, Spaghetti,' said Elvis. 'What's the problem?'

'We've just had a sighting of the **elusive** wizard, Ded Moroz. You know, the one with a long white beard, blue coat and magic crook. People say he uses it to make snow. He was with his granddaughter, the Snow Maiden. Unfortunately they got away, but we managed to fire one of our tracking devices at him. You should be picking up his location on screen now.'

Elvis switched on his **monitor** and saw a blinking red dot moving from Russia, through Belarus and Poland, across Germany and into the Netherlands.

Gosh, he's fast. He dialled up his Dutch secret agent. 'Macaroni, this is PASTA.'

'Yes, I know macaroni is pasta,' came the reply.

'No, this is Detective Elvis O'Shaughnessy, your boss, from PASTA.'

'Oh, sorry, Boss. Yes, this is Agent Macaroni. How can I help?'

'We've had a sighting of the mysterious wizard, Ded Moroz, heading in your direction with his granddaughter. They should be coming into your field of vision … about now.'

'Yes, yes,' whispered Macaroni. 'I see someone coming, but it's not Ded Moroz. It's a bearded man in a bishop's tall hat, riding a white horse. There's a wild looking half-man, half-beast with him. He's rattling chains and carrying a black bag. I recognise him. It's Black Peter, the Grumpus. And the man on the horse is Sinterklaas. They turn up every Christmas Eve to deliver presents to all the good children while the Grumpus frightens the naughty ones. But wait …'

'What?' asked Elvis.

'They've disappeared.'

I don't understand it, thought Elvis. *We started off with one supernatural sighting and now we've got two – Ded Moroz and Sinterklaas. It seems like they've both disappeared, but I've still got this red dot on my screen.* He watched it move through Belgium and France and across the sea towards England. Then it moved into Wales and across the Irish Sea.

He's heading for Ireland!

Elvis put on his coat, and grabbed his smartphone.

Outside, the air was sharp and little **flecks** of snow had started to fall.

In his car, Elvis switched on his phone and activated the app that allowed him to track the blinking red dot. It seemed to be heading for Dublin.

He slipped the phone into the cradle on his dashboard, floored the **accelerator** and **whizzed** through the empty streets. On the phone, the red dot was visiting every house in the city and in a few minutes' time the tracking device would be on the same street as Elvis.

He pulled over the car, got out and ran to the front door of the nearest house. Using his lock pick, he opened the door. Inside was warm and smelled of mince pies. In the sitting room, stockings hung over the fireplace.

When Elvis heard the faint jingle of bells somewhere up on the roof he took out his phone and prepared to call for back-up.

Suddenly, the air in the fireplace **shimmered** and then a bright flash lit up the room, dazzling Elvis.

'You're under arrest,' he said.

When he opened his eyes he saw a bearded man in a red suit, carrying a large sack.

'You … you … you're not Ded Moroz or Sinterklaas. You're Santa Claus.'

The bearded man chuckled. 'In Ireland, I'm Santa Claus, but in Russia I'm Ded Moroz and in the Netherlands I'm Sinterklaas.'

'You mean, you're the same person?'

Santa nodded. 'Why are you arresting me? Making wishes come true isn't a crime.'

Elvis's phone rang.

'Agent Tagliatelle, I'm kind of busy right now.'

'Sorry, Boss, but something big has happened up here at Loch Ness. We've captured **footage** of Nessie.'

'The Loch Ness Monster?'

'Yes, Boss, and by the way, the other secret agents and I have decided that our pasta code-names are a bit daft. So, we've all changed ours. I'm Black Eagle now.'

Elvis smiled and looked up at Santa, but the man had vanished, leaving presents where he'd been standing.

'Good work, Black Eagle,' said Elvis into the phone. 'I'll be on the next flight to Scotland.'

He opened the door and stepped out into the snowy night. Santa was right: making wishes come true was never a crime.

Kieran Fanning

A. Comprehension: Fact finding

Answer the questions.

1. What does PASTA stand for?
2. Why does Elvis want to work late?
3. How does Ded Moroz make snow, according to some people?
4. What kind of hat does Sinterklaas have?
5. What is the weather like in the story? Find a sentence that shows this.

Why does Elvis go inside the house, and how does he get in?

B. Comprehension: Read between the lines

Answer the questions.

1. Why is it odd that Elvis is at work this evening?
2. What does Agent Spaghetti mean by: 'Do you read me?'
3. Why do Ded Moroz and Sinterklaas both disappear?
4. Which part of the story do you think is funniest? Why?
5. How do you think Elvis feels at the end? Why?

What might happen at Loch Ness? Write the next part of the story.

C. Vocabulary

Choose the word or phrase that is nearest in meaning to the underlined word.

1. We heard a strange noise and went to <u>investigate</u>.
   a) escape b) look into it c) search d) hide
2. There was a <u>mysterious</u> package for me in the hallway.
   a) odd-shaped b) wrapped c) unexplained d) haunted
3. Elvis peered at the red dot on the <u>monitor</u> in disbelief.
   a) screen b) picture c) computer d) helper
4. <u>Flecks</u> of rust kept falling off my bike.
   a) lumps b) tiny flakes c) handfuls d) layers
5. The silver scales of the fish <u>shimmered</u> in the sunlight.
   a) appeared b) disappeared c) sparkled d) blazed
6. The witness used a phone to record <u>footage</u> of the getaway car.
   a) steps b) a video c) details d) information

Write two sentences about Christmas using 'shimmered' and 'mysterious'.

D. Vocabulary

Choose the most suitable word to complete each sentence.

supernatural elusive insisted whizzed accelerator operation

1. I've looked for our cat Ed everywhere, but he's very ______.
2. Lara ______ down the hill on her new bike.
3. We had to take the stairs because the lift wasn't in______.
4. I don't believe in ghosts or other ______ beings.
5. Dad ______ that we had to eat breakfast before we left.
6. Elvis stepped on the ______ and the car zoomed off.

Rewrite 4 and 5, using different words to fill the gaps.

E. Grammar: Punctuating direct speech

Direct speech is the exact words that a character says.
When writing direct speech, we always:

- Begin with a **capital letter**
- Use **speech marks**.

Speech marks (or quotation marks) are placed before and after direct speech. The speech and end punctuation always go inside the speech marks.

Examples: Cian said, 'Let's go swimming.'
'Did you hear that?' Cathy asked.

Write the sentences with speech marks.

1. Why did you do that? asked Mam.
2. I'm just off to school, said Anika.
3. Ben said, I've got a hole in my sock.
4. Stop! commanded Elvis.
5. You look ridiculous! exclaimed Melissa.
6. Have you seen my pencil case? asked Liam.

Write the sentences with correct punctuation, speech marks and capital letters.

1. how many apples have you got asked sean
2. did you do your homework asked mrs murphy
3. it's sunny today said emily
4. max said it's raining today
5. look at that said dad excitedly
6. I love christmas said molly.

Choose one of the sentences and add dialogue to continue the conversation.

F. Writing skills: Mind mapping characters

A good story always has **interesting characters**. A **mind map** is a good way to brainstorm and organise information about characters you are going to write about.

Study the mind map of Elvis O'Shaughnessy below.

Elvis O'Shaughnessy

Job: Detective

Personality: Curious, determined, hardworking, brave

Appearance: Wears a suit, trench coat and hat

Interests: Fighting supernatural threats

Choose one of these character ideas:

- ★ Santa Claus
- ★ Rudolph the red-nosed reindeer
- ★ One of Santa's elves
- ★ A snowman.

Create a mind map for your character using the headings 'Job', 'Appearance', 'Interests', 'Personality' and 'Likes/Dislikes'.

G. Writing genre: Planning a Christmas narrative

Plan a Christmas story.

1. Choose one of these story ideas, or use one of your own.
   - ★ A special Christmas wish
   - ★ When Santa caught a cold
   - ★ A funny Christmas mix-up.
2. Write the three **P**s in your copy – **P**erson, **P**lace and **P**roblem.
   - The **P**erson in your story will be the character you created a mind map for earlier.
   - Decide where your story happens and write it under **P**lace.
   - Decide what problem your character will face, and how it will be solved. Write this under **P**roblem.
3. Add some extra details to your character mind map that you can use in your story.

7b A Light in the Window

It was Christmas Eve and the dark evening sky was full of wind and rain. Miss Murtagh sighed as she lit the candle on her windowsill. She thought about the **tradition** she'd kept ever since she was a girl. Every Christmas Eve, the candle sent a message of welcome to any stranger who might be passing. 'I must be crazy,' she muttered. 'It's hardly likely anyone will even walk past my little cottage, much less stop and come in. Especially in this wild weather. But how nice it would be to have a visitor or two this Christmas ...' She turned from the window, shaking her head sadly. Then she made herself a cup of cocoa and sat watching the fire.

Miss Murtagh was just dozing off when she heard a scratching noise at the door. 'Who can that be?' she wondered. 'Probably just the wind in the branches of the tree, or the rain **battering** against the door.' Miss Murtagh peeped outside. Her eyes widened in surprise. There was a kitten on her doorstep! It was wet and thin, and mewing **pitifully**.

Without thinking twice, Miss Murtagh let the kitten in and gave it a drink of milk. It looked up gratefully as she gently stroked its head. They both settled down beside the fire. But they had only just got comfortable when there was another faint scratching at the door.

When Miss Murtagh opened the door this time, she saw a whole family of **bedraggled** field mice on the doorstep. They **trooped** in before she had time to worry about what would happen when the kitten saw them. Fortunately, there seemed to be some kind of Christmas Eve **truce**. The mice found a spot near the fire to settle. From there, they eyed the kitten **warily**. Miss Murtagh fetched them a handful of oats and they tucked in hungrily.

No sooner had Miss Murtagh got her knitting out than there was the sharp sound of barking. She opened the door to let in a vixen and her bone-thin cub. They got the remains of Miss Murtagh's supper to share. Then they too found a place by the fire.

Just as Miss Murtagh settled down again, there was a **scrabbling**, snuffling noise at the door. 'I'm not sure I've got room for many more visitors,' she fretted, 'even though it's Christmas Eve!' But she opened the door anyway. In **shuffled** an old, grey-snouted badger.

Miss Murtagh's little sitting room was getting quite full now, but the animals didn't stop coming! A family of squirrels, two ducks – even an owl decided to join the party! By the time the clock struck midnight, there was barely a **roosting** place or nesting spot free. Miss Murtagh settled back into her chair as her guests settled down for a good night's rest. She felt happy and peaceful surrounded by her Christmas visitors. Smiling, she closed her tired eyes for just a moment ...

When Miss Murtagh opened her eyes, it was Christmas morning. The storm had passed, and the candle in the window had long since gone out. The sitting room was as tidy – and empty – as ever. There was no sign of the **throng** of animals from the night before.

Perhaps I dreamed the whole thing, Miss Murtagh thought. She couldn't help feeling a little disappointed. She would be spending Christmas Day alone, and lonely, after all.

As Miss Murtagh rose to make herself a cup of tea, she heard a tiny scratching sound. At first, she thought she was hearing things, but then it came again. She went to the front door and **cautiously** eased it open.

It was the same tiny ginger kitten that had visited her in her dreams the night before. It mewed and wrapped its tiny, fluffy body around Miss Murtagh's legs. The old woman peered down the street, but there was nobody about. No mice, badgers, owls or squirrels ... and no owner in sight.

Miss Murtagh smiled and scooped the tiny creature up in her arms. Right away, it started to purr.

'You're looking for a home,' she said, 'and I've been hoping for a friend. I think we've both found what we wanted!'

Catherine Baker

A. Comprehension: Fact finding

Answer the questions.

1. When does the story take place?
2. Why does Miss Murtagh light a candle?
3. Who is her first visitor?
4. How does Miss Murtagh feel as she closes her eyes?
5. What has changed on Christmas morning?

Do you think Miss Murtagh will have a happy Christmas? Why or why not?

B. Comprehension: Read between the lines

Answer the questions.

1. Why does Miss Murtagh worry about the kitten seeing the mice?
2. How does Miss Murtagh feel when the badger arrives? Why?
3. How do we know the kitten likes Miss Murtagh?
4. Choose three words that describe Miss Murtagh's personality.
5. Do you think this is a happy story? Why or why not?

Were Miss Murtagh's visitors real or imaginary? Explain your answer.

C. Vocabulary

Choose the word or phrase that is nearest in meaning to the underlined word.

1. The stormy waves were battering the sea wall.
   a) lapping **b)** creeping to **c)** bashing **d)** flooding
2. The dog looks bedraggled because it fell in the pond.
   a) upset **b)** wet and messy **c)** tired **d)** thin
3. We all trooped in and slumped onto the sofa.
   a) crawled **b)** marched **c)** crept **d)** ran
4. Scrabbling noises were coming from the rabbits' cage.
   a) quiet **b)** running **c)** pushing **d)** scratching
5. The zombie shuffled down the road towards the town.
   a) moved slowly **b)** sprinted **c)** leaped **d)** crawled
6. A throng of children rushed into the hall for lunch.
   a) line **b)** crowd **c)** small group **d)** trio

**Which two underlined words describe walking?
Write two more words for walking.**

D. Vocabulary

Choose the most suitable word to complete each sentence.

1. It's a ______ to have turkey at Christmas. (tradition, wish, saying)
2. Our kitten whines ______ when he is hungry. (pitifully, joyously, quietly)
3. We usually argue, but we always have a ______ at Christmas. (truce, battle, present)
4. The chickens were ______ in their coop. (waking, roosting, flying)
5. I looked at the sharp knife ______. (happily, warily, helpfully)
6. She walked ______ on the icy path. (clumsily, sleepily, cautiously)

Write two new sentences using 'cautiously' and 'pitifully'.

E. Grammar: Revision – capital letters and punctuation

Write the sentences with correct capital letters and punctuation.

1. max went to the cinema on friday
2. emma and alan are going to ennis
3. have you seen the eiffel tower in paris
4. oh no max is soaking wet
5. what are you getting for christmas
6. fergus went to spain at easter
7. has anyone seen bailey today
8. did you take my green dress
9. do your exams start in july
10. i can't wait to open my presents

Write the paragraph with correct punctuation and speech marks. Start a new paragraph whenever there is a new speaker.

Don't you just love this time of year asked the Christmas tree Its so much fun being decorated with lights and baubles I feel absolutely beautiful Oh yes agreed the stocking hung by the fireplace And it's great to be out of the stuffy old attic for a while Hush the chimney whispered I think I hear Santa Claus coming

Write a short conversation between you and a friend about Christmas. Remember punctuation!

F. Writing skills: Writing character descriptions

Description can help your readers see your characters more clearly in their head. Good description also helps us understand how characters **feel**.

Example: The author tells us that Miss Murtagh **'sighed'** when she lit the candle and **'shook her head sadly'**. So we can tell that Miss Murtagh is **sad**.

Reread *A Light in the Window*. Write three details that show Miss Murtagh is a kind person.

Describe the personality and feelings of the characters in these sentences. The first has been done for you.

1. 'Get over here, you bold dog!' shouted Percy furiously.
   Percy is angry and frustrated with his naughty dog.
2. 'I'm sorry to hear that,' murmured Thomas, patting his friend gently on the arm.
3. 'I can't wait!' exclaimed Abby, bouncing up and down in excitement.
4. 'Open the door!' commanded Maggie loudly, striding towards the house.

Write a sentence with some speech that shows how these characters feel. The first has been done for you.

1. Michael is extremely hungry.
   'This soup is delicious!' said Michael, devouring his third bowlful.
2. Ben is very nervous.
3. Miss Murtagh is tired.

G. Writing genre: Writing a Christmas narrative

Use the plan you made in Unit 7a to write a Christmas story.

1. Remember to show your readers how your characters feel and what kind of personalities they have through what they do, what they say and how they say it.
2. Swap your first draft with a partner.
   - Take turns to describe the main characters in each other's stories. Does your partner see your characters the way you imagined them?
   - Give feedback to each other on how to improve your stories.
3. Write your final draft, making any improvements you can.

8a In the Wild Wind

The Wind

Listen to the wind awailing
Rattling the garden gate
Brushing the leaves of the oak tree
Rustling in the **grate**.

The cat lies flat on the hearth rug
Washing his face with his paws
The dog's asleep in the basket
Everyone's indoors.

It screams along the **alleys**
It **bellows** up the street
It groans between the gravestones
It **bowls** hats along the street.

It's **pounding** at the windows
Like the hooves of an angry horse
If it blows like this much longer
It'll knock the world **off its course**.

It's **quietened** down at bedtime
Snoring loud and deep
At six it rattles the milk crates
And finally falls asleep.

Gareth Owen

The Whisper-Whisper Man

The Whisper-Whisper Man
Makes all the wind in the world.
He has a gown as brown as brown:
His hair is long and curled.

In the stormy wintertime
He taps at your windowpane.
And all the night, until it's light,
He whispers through the rain.

If you peeped through a Fairy Ring
You'd see him, little and brown;
You'd hear the beat of his clackety feet
Scampering through the town.

Anonymous

A. Comprehension: Fact finding

Answer the questions.

1. In 'The Wind', what noise does the wind make in the grate?
2. Name two animals who are inside the house in 'The Wind'.
3. In 'The Wind', what noise does the wind make in the graveyard?
4. What is the Whisper-Whisper Man's job?
5. What would you have to do to see the Whisper-Whisper Man?

In 'The Wind', why is a horse mentioned? Is there a real horse? Give reasons.

B. Comprehension: Read between the lines

Answer the questions.

1. What three verbs do you find most descriptive in 'The Wind'? Why?
2. In verse two of 'The Wind', why do you think 'everyone's indoors'?
3. Write a sentence describing the Whisper-Whisper Man.
4. Is the 'Whisper-Whisper Man' a good name for the character? Why?
5. Which poem makes the wind sound louder? Explain your answer.

Which of the two poems do you prefer? Explain your choice.

C. Vocabulary

Choose the word or phrase that is nearest in meaning to the underlined word or phrase.

1. A big log was burning brightly in the <u>grate</u>.
   a) garden **b)** room **c)** bonfire **d)** fireplace
2. My brother <u>bellows</u> when he doesn't get his way.
   a) sulks **b)** weeps **c)** shouts **d)** complains
3. In high winds, trampolines can <u>bowl</u> over.
   a) slither **b)** roll **c)** skid **d)** thud
4. I heard someone <u>pounding</u> at the door.
   a) tapping **b)** hammering **c)** pushing **d)** opening
5. My toboggan went <u>off its course</u> and hit a tree.
   a) the wrong way **b)** right **c)** left **d)** sideways
6. The puppy went <u>scampering</u> across the field.
   a) pounding **b)** walking **c)** plodding **d)** scurrying

Think of two more words that have a similar meaning to 'pounding'.

D. Vocabulary

Choose the most suitable words from the box to complete the paragraph

rattling alleys rustling quietened pounding

Yesterday, a fierce wind blew down the streets and _______ as I walked home. It was _______ the leaves of the oak trees. The breeze made a _______ noise as it shook the windows of the houses. I ran home as fast as I could, my feet _______ on the pavement. By the time I reached home, the noisy, blustery wind had finally calmed and _______ down.

Write a sentence about a windy afternoon. Use some words from the box.

E. Grammar: Plural nouns (part 1)

Remember: **nouns** are naming words.

Examples: car, bus, baby.

To make most nouns plural, add -s.	**Examples:** cars, horses, bulls.
If the noun ends in -s, -x, -ch or -sh, add -es.	**Examples:** buses, foxes, watches.
If the noun ends in a consonant + -y, replace the *y* with *ie* and add -s.	**Examples:** babies, parties.

Write the sentences, turning the underlined singular nouns into plurals.

1. We took the sick cat to see the vet.
2. The girl ate the apple from the tree.
3. The toddler unwrapped the box and took out the toy bus.
4. The boy found the coat under the bush.
5. The family got into the car and drove to their house.

Write the plurals of each of these nouns.

Find two plural nouns in 'The Wind' and use each one in a sentence.

F. Writing skills: Similes and metaphors

A **simile** compares two things using 'like' or 'as'. Writers use similes to create pictures in readers' minds.

Example: The ice shone **like** diamonds.

Find and write a simile used in 'The Wind'.

Complete these similes with your own ideas.

- The wind howled like ...
- The puddles were as deep as ...

Metaphors compare two things *without* using the words 'like' or 'as'. They are often used in poems.

Example: The moon **is a** silver coin.

Write the meanings of these metaphors in your copy.

- The storm was a ferocious beast.
- Our aunt is a dragon.
- My sister is a beam of sunshine.

G. Writing genre: Planning a weather poem

Plan a poem about the weather.

1. Choose a kind of weather to write about. It could be sun, hail, snow, a thunderstorm or something else.
2. Answer these questions in your copy:
   - What are the best and worst things about this type of weather?
   - What would you **feel**, **see**, **hear**, **smell** and perhaps even **taste** in this weather?
   - What emotions does it make you feel?
3. Turn your notes into a mind map like this one.

4. Add some similes and metaphors about your weather to your mind map.

Examples: The fog **is a** thick, cold blanket. **(metaphor)**
The fog is **as** thick **as** pea soup. **(simile)**

8b Describing the Rain

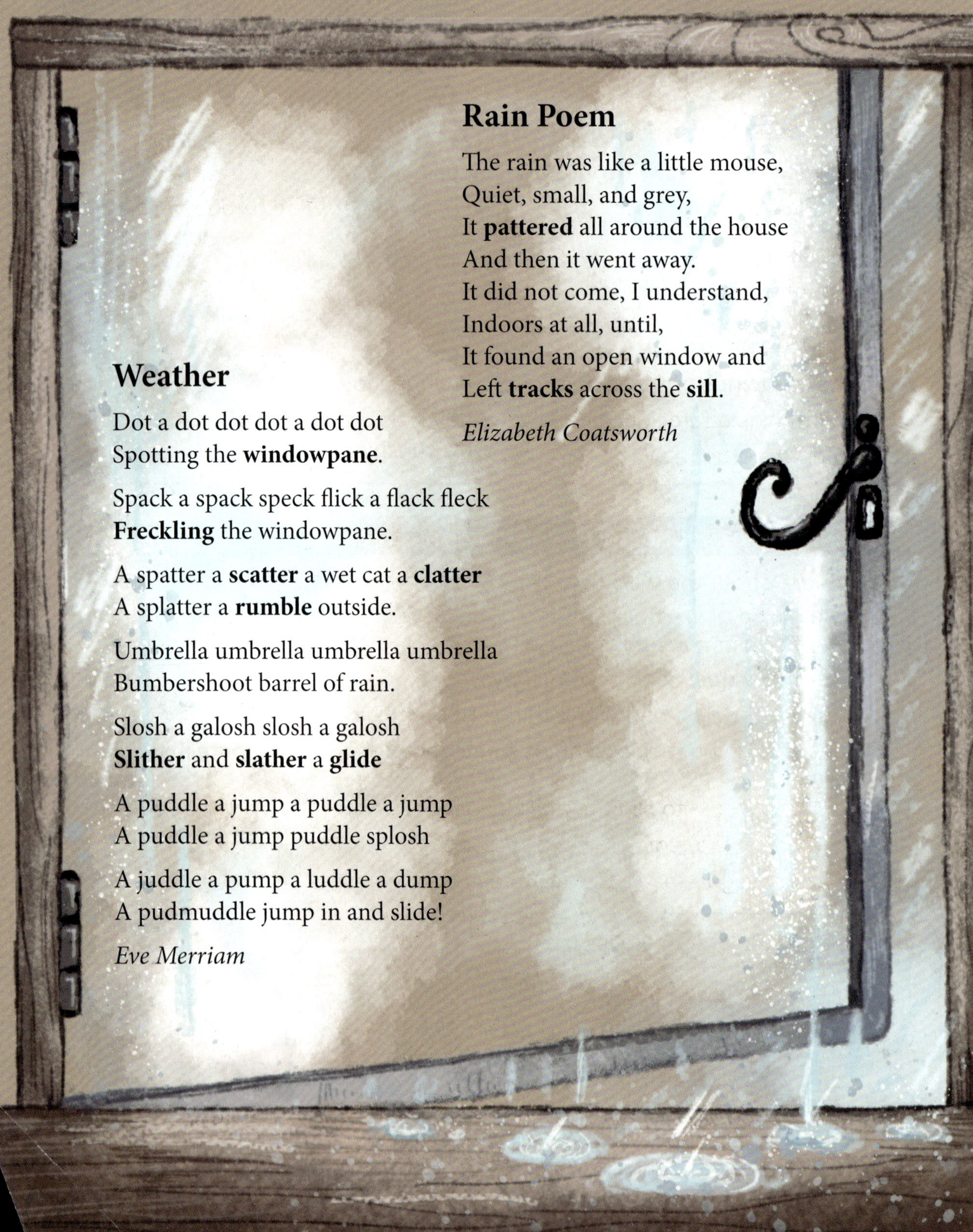

Rain Poem

The rain was like a little mouse,
Quiet, small, and grey,
It **pattered** all around the house
And then it went away.
It did not come, I understand,
Indoors at all, until,
It found an open window and
Left **tracks** across the **sill**.

Elizabeth Coatsworth

Weather

Dot a dot dot dot a dot dot
Spotting the **windowpane**.

Spack a spack speck flick a flack fleck
Freckling the windowpane.

A spatter a **scatter** a wet cat a **clatter**
A splatter a **rumble** outside.

Umbrella umbrella umbrella umbrella
Bumbershoot barrel of rain.

Slosh a galosh slosh a galosh
Slither and **slather** a **glide**

A puddle a jump a puddle a jump
A puddle a jump puddle splosh

A juddle a pump a luddle a dump
A pudmuddle jump in and slide!

Eve Merriam

A. Comprehension: Fact finding

Answer the questions.

1. In 'Rain Poem', what does the poet compare the rain to?
2. In 'Rain Poem', how does the rain get inside the house?
3. In 'Weather', what animal does the poet mention?
4. What are the last two verses of 'Weather' about?
5. What is the name of the poet who wrote 'Weather'?

Think of a different title for 'Rain Poem'.

B. Comprehension: Read between the lines

Answer the questions.

1. How can we tell the rain had come indoors in 'Rain Poem'?
2. Does 'Rain Poem' describe the rain well? Explain your answer.
3. What do you think the 'rumble outside' in 'Weather' might be?
4. How does the poet of 'Weather' feel about the rain? How do you know?
5. Which of these two rain poems do you like best? Why?

What do you think the word 'bumbershoot' might mean in 'Weather'?

C. Vocabulary

Choose the word or phrase that is nearest in meaning to the underlined word.

1. There were paper clips <u>scattered</u> all over the floor.
   a) hidden **b)** sprinkled **c)** piled **d)** collected
2. The snake started to <u>slither</u> into the bushes.
   a) slide **b)** disappear **c)** race **d)** scatter
3. The swans began to <u>glide</u> gracefully across the lake.
   a) swim **b)** fly **c)** pass **d)** slide smoothly
4. Dad likes to <u>slather</u> his apple crumble in custard.
   a) cook **b)** cover **c)** dab **d)** eat
5. The kitten's tiny paws <u>pattered</u> across the floor.
   a) rolled **b)** slid **c)** stepped quickly **d)** thumped
6. We saw the muddy <u>tracks</u> that Buddy had left on the floor.
   a) footprints **b)** holes **c)** lines **d)** sticks

Which underlined words describe movement? Use one in a senten

D. Vocabulary

Choose the most suitable word to complete each sentence.

sill windowpane freckling clatter rumble

1. Suddenly we heard the _______ of thunder in the distance.
2. There was a small vase of flowers on the _______.
3. Annie dropped her tray with a loud _______.
4. There were small brown spots _______ the puppy's fur.
5. I could hardly see through the dirty _______.

Which two words describe sounds? Think of three more sound words.

E. Grammar: Plural nouns (part 2)

Remember: most nouns are made plural by adding -s or -es.

Some nouns have **irregular plurals**. These are made by changing the word, adding a different ending, or simply not changing anything!

Examples:

Singular	man	louse	wolf	foot	sheep
Plural	men	lice	wolves	feet	sheep

Write the plurals of these irregular nouns.

1. hoof
2. child
3. leaf
4. mouse
5. tooth
6. person
7. elf
8. deer

Write the sentences, turning the singular nouns into plurals. The first one has been done for you.

1. The child ate their sandwich and crisp.
   The children ate their sandwiches and crisps.
2. The horse thundered past, their hoof splashing through the puddle.
3. Please get the loaf down from the shelf so the girl can have their lunch.
4. The wizard locked their wand in the iron box.
5. Did you see the mouse hiding inside the pepper?
6. I love jumping in muddy puddle and listening to thunderstorm.

List some of your favourite things, using plural nouns.

F. Writing skills: Using imaginative words

Poets often use words that help us **imagine** what they are writing about.

Example: In 'Rain Poem', the words 'quiet' and 'pattered' help us imagine the rain as a little mouse.

Find two other words in 'Rain Poem' that help you imagine the rain as a mouse.

Each of these sentences helps us imagine the rain is like an animal. Write:

1. What you think each animal is
2. What words made you imagine that.

- The rain slithered and twisted down the windowpane.
- The rain hopped and jumped as it bounced off the pavement.
- The rain tickled and prickled as it ran down my neck!

G. Writing genre: Writing a weather poem

Use the mind map you made in Unit 8a to write a weather poem.

1. Write your first draft. Remember to:
   - Describe how the weather makes you feel.
   - Include what you see, hear, smell, feel and taste.
   - Use some words that help the reader imagine the weather you are writing about.
   - Include a metaphor or simile that compares the weather to something else.
2. Read your first draft out loud to a partner.
   - Does it sound good and make sense?
   - Can you swap any of your words for more interesting ones?
3. Write a final draft of your poem, making any improvements you can.

9a A New Life for Leila

10 February 2016

Hello! My name is Leila and I am 10 years old. I live in Galway now, but once I lived in Syria, in a city called Aleppo. I want to tell you all about my journey to where I am today.

You might have heard of Aleppo because of the war there. I wish you could have seen my beautiful city before the war began! In my memory, the sun was always shining, and home was full of laughter, love and delicious smells of cooking. The streets were always so busy and full of life. The day the bomb hit our **apartment**, all of that ended. Even my family is smaller now – just my mum and me. Life is colder now, and quieter. But at least we still have love – and cooking.

After our apartment was destroyed, Mum and I **escaped** to Turkey. Many other people from Syria were doing the same thing. We lived in a camp with thousands of other **refugees**. We lived in tents **crammed** closely together. Some people got ill because of dirty water and unsafe food. It seemed a long while that we lived in that camp. At last, one day, Mum told me we were leaving. Almost before I knew what was happening, I found myself on a plane heading to Ireland.

At first, I found my new life in Galway strange. Compared with Syria and Turkey, Ireland seemed so cold. I had never dreamed it could rain so much! But we were very glad to be away from the war and to be safe. Most of the people we met were kind to us – although, sometimes we met people who were not so kind. A woman at a bus stop once told us to 'go back home'. I was upset, because my old home has gone forever. If Galway is not my home now, then I have no home.

When I started at school, it was hard. Everything was so different from my old school in Aleppo. I didn't even speak much English at first, and soon I discovered that I would need to learn Irish too! I felt **confused** and lonely. But most of the children in my class were nice, and before long I made a good friend, Cara. We like the same things – music, animals and drawing! I didn't need much English or Irish to share those things with Cara.

After a while, my English started improving. There were special classes, and I picked up new words quickly. Maybe it helped that I knew several languages already – Arabic, French and some Turkish. So adding a new language wasn't so hard.

Soon, I started feeling happier, but I was still worried about my mum. She was looking for a job, but her English was not good, so it was difficult. In the evenings, she was too sad and tired to cook much. We ate a lot of soft, **bland** bread, and hummus from a supermarket tub.

Then, one day Mum bought lamb mince and bulgur wheat and spices. She made some kibbeh that tasted just as good as the ones I remember, back in Aleppo! I took the leftovers into school the next day in my packed lunch. My teacher, Mrs Cooper, noticed me eating them. 'Those look delicious, Leila!' she said. 'Do you mind if I try one?'

Kibbeh

Mrs Cooper liked the kibbeh so much that they gave her an idea. 'Do you think your mum would come in and talk to us about Syrian food, Leila?' she asked. 'It would link so well with our project on food around the world!'

I smiled, and said I'd ask, but secretly I felt **doubtful**. Mum's English was not good, and perhaps she was too sad and tired to come into school.

To my surprise, Mum was pleased! She said that she would come into school if I would help her with the talking. 'And we will do more than talk, Leila,' she said. 'We will let the children taste our Syrian food!'

For days **beforehand**, Mum was busy cooking. She bustled around the kitchen, humming to herself as she **ground** spices. She smiled as she sniffed the **fragrant** air above her saucepan.

When the day arrived, we had so much food to share with the class! Mum had made her special kibbeh, a delicious **tangy** flatbread called manoushi, and a **rich**, creamy dessert called kanafeh, which is a bit like cheesecake. There was enough for everyone to try. I helped her explain what everything was, and how it was made.

Manoushi
Kanafeh

Afterwards, I felt so proud of my mum. Since then, things have started to improve for her. She has found a job in a local cafe, cooking Syrian pastries. People come from miles around to taste them! And that's not all. Last week, Mum even made a batch of pickles. This is a small thing, but important – because pickles mean home. You only make pickles when you know you are staying to eat them. Perhaps this means that Mum and I have stopped travelling for now. Perhaps Galway is really our home.

A. Comprehension: Fact finding

Answer the questions.

1. What is the name of the city where Leila used to live?
2. Why did Leila and her mum have to go to Turkey?
3. Name one way Leila's life in Galway seemed strange at first.
4. Who is Leila's friend in school, and what do they have in common?
5. What idea did Mrs Cooper have when she tasted the kibbeh?

Do you think Leila was happy that her mum made pickles? Why?

B. Comprehension: Read between the lines

Answer the questions.

1. Describe Leila's feelings about her old home in Aleppo.
2. Why was Leila upset when someone told her to go back home?
3. How do you think Leila felt when her mum made some kibbeh?
4. Why was Leila surprised when her mum agreed to come to school?
5. Why did Leila feel proud of her mum?

Imagine you are in Leila's class. How could you help her feel welcome?

C. Vocabulary

Choose the word or phrase that is nearest in meaning to the underlined word.

1. Uncle Cillian lives in an apartment near the town centre.
   a) area **b)** small house **c)** flat **d)** mansion
2. Twenty teddies are crammed into my bed.
   a) arranged **b)** packed tightly **c)** heaped **d)** thrown
3. I tried to read the map but it made me feel confused.
   a) puzzled **b)** dizzy **c)** annoyed **d)** homesick
4. Dad was doubtful we'd get home on time.
   a) scared **b)** hopeful **c)** optimistic **d)** uncertain
5. We didn't take a picnic because we'd eaten beforehand.
   a) heartily **b)** earlier **c)** afterwards **d)** a lot
6. My Granny's garden is full of fragrant flowers.
   a) colourful **b)** fragile **c)** scented **d)** large

Write a sentence about a food you like, using 'fragrant'.

D. Vocabulary

Choose the most suitable word to complete each sentence.

1. They were lucky to ______ the war. (see, experience, escape)
2. People who leave their homes because of war are ______.
   (refugees, confused, doubtful)
3. Porridge is quite a ______ food. (tangy, bland, fragrant)
4. The smell of ______ coffee is very strong. (ground, fragrant, bland)
5. My favourite drink is fizzy, ______ lemonade. (creamy, bland, tangy)
6. Chocolate cake is delicious but very ______. (tangy, rich, bland)

Make a list of tangy foods and a list of bland foods.

E. Grammar: Verbs

Verbs are doing words. Examples: walk, climb.

We add **-ed** to put verbs in the **past tense**.

Examples: I **walked** downstairs. He **climbed** the tree.

Some verbs are irregular. The past tense for these verbs is made in different ways.

Examples: **get → got**; **see → saw**; **run → ran**; **have → had**; **is → was.**

Write the paragraph with all the verbs in the past tense.

I pick up my coat and bag, and run out the door. I am in a massive hurry because the bus is almost at the bus stop. I feel out of breath by the time I get there. Luckily, the driver sees me. He waves and waits for me. My friend Sam laughs at me, but I am not cross. I am so happy that I am not late.

To put verbs in the **future tense**, we use '**will**'.

Examples: I **will** play after school. I **will** walk the dog later.

Write the sentences in the future tense. The last one is irregular.

1. I wait for the bus.
2. I play a game with my friend.
3. I eat dinner with my family.
4. I am tired after swimming.

How many verbs can you think of that don't use -ed in the past tense? Write a list.

F. Writing skills: Who, what, when and where

Recounts usually have an opening that tells us **who** the recount is about, **when** the events happened and **where**. Recounts tell us **what** happened, usually in the order that the events happened.

Read this short recount, then follow the instructions below.

Leaving Dublin

Last August, my Mam told me we were going to move from Dublin to Portlaoise. At first, I was really upset that I would have to leave my school and all my friends. Two weeks later, a moving van came and the movers put all our furniture inside. Then my Mam, Dad, brother and I drove to our new home. While we were unpacking, our neighbours came over to say hello. There was a girl my age called Abigail. We became friends right away. Finally, I started to think that I might like it in Portlaoise.

1. Find an example of these features of a recount in the text above. Write them in your copy.

title | time words | ending | when? | where? | what happened? | who?

2. Now find an example of each feature in *A New Life for Leila.*

G. Writing genre: Planning a recount of a journey

Plan a recount about a journey you have made.

1. Think about a journey you took in the past.
   - Tell a partner what happened. Give as much detail as you can.
   - Ask your partner about their journey. Make your questions as interesting and detailed as possible.
   - Talk about how you felt at each stage of the journey.
2. Make notes about what happened and how you felt. Use a plan like this one.

Going to Granny's on the train				
What happened	Granny arrived at my house	Together we went to the station	I read my book on the train	We arrived at Granny's house
How I felt	A bit sad to leave home	Excited to get on the train	Relaxed and happy	A bit tired and very hungry!

9b Michael's Workhouse Diary

The first workhouses opened in Ireland in the early 1840s and they lasted until the 1920s. At this time, many people were struggling to find jobs or earn enough to live on. The workhouses offered a place where poor families could come to live and could receive some food in return for work.

Workhouses were not ***pleasant*** *places to live, but many desperate families felt that they had no* ***alternative****. In this diary* ***extract****, Michael tells the story of how he came to live in the workhouse, and what life was like there.*

24 October 1848

Today we left our home – the cottage I love, where I've lived since I was born. Father says we have no choice. The little money that he can earn is not enough to feed us all. The famine has made food so **scarce**, and what little food there is costs so much now! I felt like crying when we closed the door behind us for the last time and **walked** down the road to town. But I didn't let myself cry, because I'd promised Mother that I would be brave, for the sake of the little ones.

When we reached the workhouse, I felt even worse. I'd seen its high dark walls before, of course, but now we were going to see them from the inside. The doors **slammed** shut behind us, but then a worse shock awaited us! We were to be **separated**. The Matron, a large, cross-looking woman, came **striding** up to us and ordered Father to the men's quarters. Mother and Mary-Ann, the baby, were sent to the women's quarters. We older children were sharply told to run along to the boys' and girls' **dormitories**. I hope I'll be **permitted** to see my parents and sisters tomorrow. But Patrick, another boy in my dormitory, has told me that this is forbidden by strict **command** of the workhouse Master. I hope he's lying!

25 October 1848

It's been a long day today! I'm grateful to have a quiet moment to write in my diary. There are hundreds of rules in this workhouse, so we never seem to get a minute to ourselves. This morning, we rose at seven. I quickly dressed myself in the rough, scratchy clothes I've been given. Then we trooped down to the dining hall in our groups – first the girls, then the boys, then the women and finally the men. We were all kept separate. Patrick was right – there was no chance of seeing the rest of my family.

Down in the dining room, we had to sit through lots of prayers before we were allowed a scrap of breakfast. One of the workhouse staff checked that we were clean. Then finally, we picked up our cups and plates and lined up to collect a drink of milk and a ladleful of stirabout – a sort of thin porridge. We ate in complete silence.

After we'd eaten breakfast, we children were meant to have lessons. But there is only one schoolteacher in this workhouse, and over 300 children. The teacher is a **mean** elderly man who raises his voice and **waves** a cane about but he is completely **incapable** of keeping order. I managed to find a seat in the schoolroom, but I didn't learn much in his lesson. Patrick decided not to bother with the lesson, but one of the workhouse staff spotted him in the corridor. As a punishment, he was sent to sit all by himself in a dark room with no windows for the rest of the day. He was lucky they didn't beat him.

When lesson time was over, we were made to work. Girls had to **assist** with the cleaning, and we boys were sent to work in the workhouse garden. At least we got to see some daylight out there! After that, we were made to help turn the capstan wheel. This is a massive stone wheel for grinding corn. You have to walk round and round in circles pushing the wheel. It was very tiring, thirsty and hungry work.

There was no food between breakfast and dinner, even though we were all so hungry from working. Dinner wasn't until late afternoon, and it was just thin soup and **coarse** brown bread. Still, I can't really complain, much as I disliked it – it's not as if we had more than this to eat back at home.

Bedtime was eight o'clock for everyone – men, women and children. By then, I was so **exhausted** and hungry that I fell asleep at once.

I'm not going to stay in this workhouse forever. When the famine is over, I'll leave and get a job on a farm, or over in Galway. Or maybe I'll **emigrate** to America – they say there's a good living to be made over there. Whatever happens, I'm going to make enough money to buy a house for my family, where we can all live together and be happy. I just need to stay out of trouble and keep my wits about me until that time comes.

A. Comprehension: Fact finding

Answer the questions.

1. Why did Michael's family have to go to the workhouse?
2. Why didn't Michael cry when they left home?
3. What must the boys do after lessons?
4. How many meals a day do they have in the workhouse?
5. What does Michael hope to do in the future?

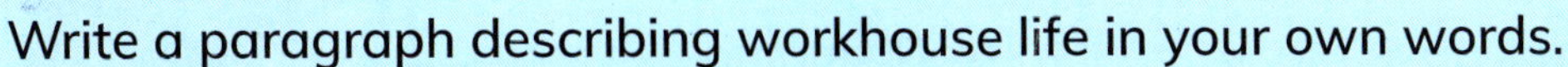

Write a paragraph describing workhouse life in your own words.

B. Comprehension: Read between the lines

Answer the questions.

1. If workhouses were so unpleasant, why did people go there?
2. Why do you think conditions were poor in workhouses?
3. What does Michael call a 'worse shock'? Why is it worse?
4. Would you like to eat stirabout? Why or why not?
5. Who do you think had the worst jobs – girls or boys? Why?

Do you think you would learn much in the workhouse? Why or why not?

C. Vocabulary

Choose the word or phrase that is nearest in meaning to the underlined word.

1. We read an extract from one of the *Harry Potter* books.
   a) sentence **b)** review **c)** short section **d)** diary
2. The Wall Brown butterfly is scarce in most of Ireland.
   a) banned **b)** found **c)** common **d)** rare
3. Jack and his friends got separated at the fair.
   a) split up **b)** fed up **c)** annoyed **d)** cheated
4. I'm not permitted to walk home after dark.
   a) scared **b)** allowed **c)** able **d)** keen
5. Mam was feeling exhausted so she went to bed.
   a) ill **b)** extremely tired **c)** miserable **d)** very happy
6. Children used to wear clothes made of coarse cloth.
   a) nasty **b)** woven **c)** rough **d)** thick

Write a sentence about a time when you felt exhausted.

D. Vocabulary

Choose the most suitable word to complete each sentence.

pleasant slammed assist incapable emigrate command

1. Many Irish people decided to ______ to the United States.
2. Dad asked me to ______ with making the dinner.
3. Eating snails isn't very ______ , in my opinion.
4. After our argument, my sister ______ the door.
5. Our principal gave the ______ to start singing.
6. My little brother is ______ of tying his shoelaces.

Write one sentence using two of the words from the box.

E. Grammar: More homophones

Remember: **homophones** are words that sound the same but have different spellings and meanings.

Examples: Jay is **eight** years old. We **ate** a pizza.

Write the sentences with the correct homophones.

1. We had a picnic in the ______ . (would/wood)
2. Mam had packed ______ sandwiches and cake. (sum/some)
3. Did you get the answers ______ ? (right/write)
4. Of ______ you can come! (coarse/course)
5. I'd like to ______ a new pencil case. (by/buy)
6. I wonder ______ it's going to snow? (whether/weather)
7. I don't like ______ in my sandwiches. (meat/meet)
8. There's a massive ______ in the road. (whole/hole)

Write homophones for these words.

hear piece site bee our knight threw

Choose one of your homophone pairs and write a sentence for each word.

right write would wood by buy

F. Writing skills: Adding interesting details

Read this first draft of a recount.

My first plane trip

We went on holiday to Spain last year. I had never been on a plane before that.

On the morning of the plane trip we had to get up very early. It was a long car ride to the airport. When we got there, it was still early but the airport was very busy.

We had to wait ages until it was time to get on the plane. I was surprised how big the plane was. The flight was about three hours long. It was a bit bumpy when we landed. I enjoyed my first plane trip.

1. Imagine it is your recount. Make up details to make it more interesting. Include:
   - Who else went on the trip with you
   - How you felt
   - What else you saw and heard in the airport and on the plane
   - What was fun about the flight.
2. Write a new draft, including the new details. Start a new paragraph for each new thing that happens.

G. Writing genre: Writing a recount of a journey

Use the plan you made in Unit 9a to write a recount of a journey you went on.

1. Write your first draft. Remember to:
   - Write what happened in chronological order.
   - Start a new paragraph for each new thing that happens.
   - Tell the reader how you felt about the journey.
2. Read your work. Is it interesting? Could you add any more details?
3. Write your second draft, making any improvements you can.

10a Comparing Lives

Introduction

This report compares the lives of three children who live in very different places. Singapore, where Alicia lives, is a bustling island city. The part of India where Nandi lives is very rural (though many other Indian children live in cities). James's life in the Australian **outback** is unlike that of children who live in big Australian cities such as Sydney or Adelaide. Your life might seem like a big **contrast** to theirs, or maybe you've got more in common than you might think?

Home life

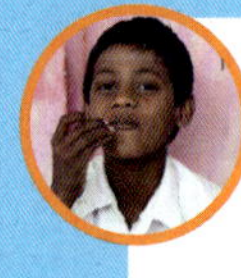

Nandi lives in a small village in the state of Bihar, north-east India. He lives in a mud-brick house with his mam and dad, his brothers Aditya and Arjun and his sister Anaya. The family's farm is about half the size of a football pitch. They grow vegetables such as potatoes, onions and cauliflowers. They also have some cows, which they keep for milk. Nandi shares a bedroom with the other children.

Alicia lives with her mam and dad in a big apartment block in Singapore. Singapore is a city that is also an island. Over five million people live there, so it's quite **congested**. Alicia's flat is small, but she has her own bedroom. They don't have a garden.

James lives on his family's cattle farm in the Australian outback, nearly 150 km from the nearest town. James and his sister, Marina, have plenty of outdoor space to play in, but there aren't many other children living nearby. Their house is big, with a shady, covered area called a **veranda** running all around it.

School

It's an early start every morning for Alicia, as school begins at 7.20 a.m. However, it's hometime at 1.40 p.m. Alicia's school is quite strict and **academic**. The children have to take tough exams in English, Maths and Science before they leave primary school. So Alicia goes to after-school classes in Maths and English to help her **excel** in the exams.

In Nandi's school, children of different ages study together. The teacher, Mr Prakash, is helpful but there are not many books. Nandi's parents want him to do well at school so that he will have a chance of getting a good job. Nandi would like to be a doctor when he grows up, so he is studying hard.

James doesn't have to leave his house to go to school! His farm is too **remote** to travel there and back every day. Instead, he and Marina learn at home using materials provided by an **organisation** called the School of the Air. They get some lessons through the post, and every day they have at least one lesson online. This is an **opportunity** to chat with the teacher and other children. Their teacher uses the internet to give them help and support, and their mam and dad **ensure** they spend plenty of time studying on their own too.

Chores

James helps his mam and dad look after the cattle on their farm, and it's his special job to look after the chickens. He wakes early every morning so he can feed them and let them out of their coop.

Alicia has to help keep the flat tidy. She makes her bed every morning, and sets the table. Sometimes she does jobs such as dusting the shelves, for extra pocket money!

Nandi has lots of **chores** to do to help his family grow food. His day starts early, long before school begins. He waters the crops and helps to milk the cows.

Food and fun

James and Marina enjoy playing together outdoors and swimming in the local creek. When the family travels into the local town every few weeks, they enjoy going to the cinema and bowling alley and meeting up with friends. The family has to think ahead about food because there are no shops nearby. They keep lots of food in the freezer. It's not much fun running out of food when you can't just pop to the shops!

All the children in Nandi's school enjoy playing cricket. They've turned an area behind the school into a cricket pitch. Nandi's family eat the vegetables they grow on their farm, with rice or chapatis (a sort of flat bread). They also like sattu, which is a porridge made from ground grains and **pulses**. If they have a bad year on the farm, there may not be enough to eat. But in Nandi's village, everyone helps each other, so neighbours share food when times are tough.

Alicia has a big choice of things to do in Singapore. There are lots of cinemas, museums, water parks and playgrounds. But what Alicia likes best is spending time with her school friends. Alicia's family sometimes eats in local restaurants, but the food Alicia really loves best is homemade chicken and rice with chilli and soy sauce.

Things to think about

How does your life compare to James's, Nandi's and Alicia's? What is the same and what is different? Would you want to swap lives with any of these children?

A. Comprehension: Fact finding

Answer the questions.

1. Which country does Nandi live in?
2. Which of the children does **not** live on a farm?
3. What does Alicia do to help her do well in her exams?
4. Why doesn't James travel to school?
5. What does Nandi have to do before he goes to school?

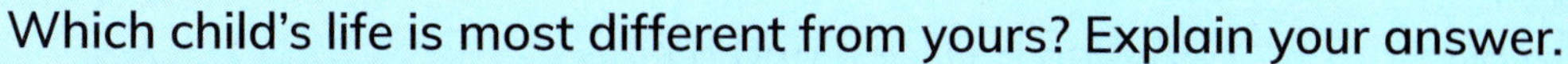

Which child's life is most different from yours? Explain your answer.

B. Comprehension: Read between the lines

Answer the questions.

1. How might Alicia feel if she swapped places with James?
2. Why must everyone help each other in Nandi's village?
3. Why does James's family need a big freezer?
4. Name one good thing and one bad thing about each child's life.
5. Which of the three children would you most like to visit? Why?

Why do you think the author chose these three places?

C. Vocabulary

Choose the word or phrase that is nearest in meaning to the underlined word.

1. At rush hour, the roads are congested.
   a) ugly **b)** modern **c)** crowded **d)** narrow
2. I excel at making chocolate cake.
   a) do well **b)** fail **c)** struggle **d)** attempt
3. My cousins live in a remote village in Donegal.
   a) isolated **b)** beautiful **c)** interesting **d)** lonely
4. Aiden hoped there would be an opportunity to play football.
   a) reason **b)** minute **c)** place **d)** chance
5. Mam ensures we dress warmly in winter.
   a) makes certain **b)** hopes **c)** prefers **d)** requests
6. We finished our chores before lunchtime.
   a) snacks **b)** jobs **c)** homework **d)** reading

Use the word 'remote' to describe a place in Ireland.

D. Vocabulary

Choose the most suitable word to complete each sentence.

academic contrast pulses organisation outback veranda

1. My cousin's school is quite _______, so she gets lots of homework.
2. Many children in the Australian _______ do not travel to school.
3. Scouts is an _______ that encourages young people to be active.
4. I'm not keen on most _______, but I do like baked beans.
5. There's a big _______ between a village and a city.
6. When it's hot outside, we sit on our shady _______.

Write sentences about two contrasting places.

E. Grammar: Conjunctions of time

Conjunctions join parts of a sentence or two sentences together.
Conjunctions of time help us work out *when* things happened.

Examples: We were walking home **when** we saw Sarah.
Sam was hungry **after** digging in the garden all morning.

Write the paragraph using one of the conjunctions of time to fill each gap.

when after before while

Saoirse had just stepped outside _______ she stopped in surprise. It was a few moments _______ she could take in what she was looking at. She was surrounded by an unfamiliar snowy landscape. A line of penguins shuffled past her, _______ a family of seals lolloped across the ice. 'I must be dreaming,' Saoirse said to herself, _______ a polar bear skated past. 'This wasn't here this morning!'

Write the sentences, adding more information after the conjunctions.

1. Remember to brush your teeth before ...
2. I'll wait with you until ...
3. Harry and Ronan have been playing football since ...

Write sentences using the conjunctions 'before' and 'after'.

F. Writing skills: Editing

We **edit** our writing to improve it and make it clearer for the reader. We also add interesting details and fix mistakes.

A **first draft** is your first attempt at a piece of writing. A **final draft** is the final version. Final drafts have been edited, proofread and rewritten.

Read this first draft of a report about the Forbidden City.

The Forbidden City is located in Beijing. It was the palace of the Chinese emperors during the Ming and Qing Dynasties. It is the largest ancient palace in the world. It has 980 buildings with at least 8,700 rooms. The Forbidden Palace was very expensive to build. The best materials were brought from all over China.

Write the second draft of this report in your copy.

1. Give it a title.
2. Start a new paragraph whenever there is a new topic.
3. Add the details in the box below into the appropriate paragraph.

- Beijing is the capital city of China.
- The Forbidden City covers an area of 178 acres.
- Specially made 'golden' bricks were used in the construction.

G. Writing genre: Planning a report

Plan a report about life in another country.

1. Choose three of these topics to write about:
   - ★ Daily life in that country
   - ★ An interesting place to visit there
   - ★ Animals who live in that country
   - ★ School in that country
   - ★ Food in that country.
2. Make a KWL chart about the country you have chosen.
   - Write what you already know about it in the **K** column.
   - Write all the things you want to know in the **W** column.
   - Use books and the internet to research the answers to your questions. Write the answers in the **L** column.

10b Helping the World's Poorest Children

Wherever they live around the world, all children have the same basic needs and rights. Here are some of the most important things all children should have for a happy and healthy life:

- **Nutritious** food and water that is safe to drink
- **Access** to healthcare if they are ill
- A safe place to live, with their own family if possible
- A peaceful place to live, where life isn't threatened by other people
- A good education
- Opportunities to play and to rest.

Unfortunately, not all children have all these things. In fact, some children who live with war, famine or natural disasters have *none* of these things.

Looking out for children

So who helps these children? Sometimes **governments** help by providing education and healthcare, and by making sure that adults have enough money to support their families. But sometimes governments in **developing** countries aren't able to help, because they don't have enough money. If a big natural disaster affects thousands of people in a developing country, for example, the government might not be able to help all these people.

This is where **development** charities come in. These are charities that work to support people in the poorest communities all around the world. There are lots of development charities based in Ireland, but one of the best-known is Trócaire.

What does Trócaire do?

Trócaire was founded in 1973 by the Catholic Church in Ireland. It has two main aims:

- To support the most **vulnerable** people in the developing world
- To raise awareness in Ireland about poverty and **injustice** around the world.

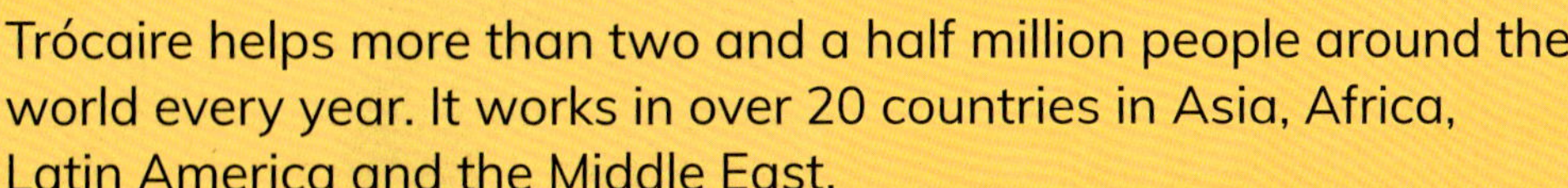

Trócaire helps more than two and a half million people around the world every year. It works in over 20 countries in Asia, Africa, Latin America and the Middle East.

Here's just a flavour of the work Trócaire does to help poor and vulnerable people around the world.

Nepal: In 2015, a huge earthquake struck, killing nearly 9,000 people and destroying many thousands of homes. Trócaire immediately sent teams of specialist workers to help local people cope with the **aftermath** of the disaster. Several years later, Trócaire is still working in the region to help people rebuild their homes and lives.

South Sudan: In this extremely poor and **war-torn** country, Trócaire helps thousands of people who have lost their homes because of the continuing war.

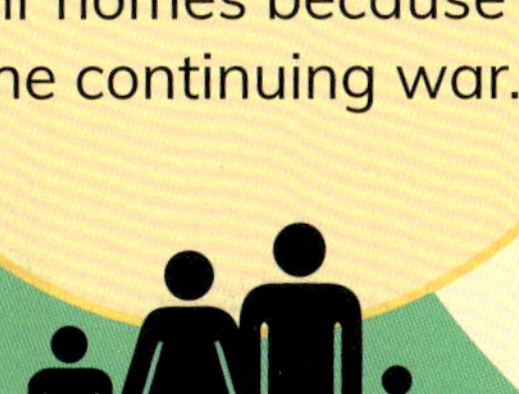

Syria: Over half the people of Syria have been forced to leave their homes because of war. Many of these people are living in refugee camps in other countries. Trócaire provides food, shelter and other support to thousands of Syrian refugees.

Where does the money come from?

People in Ireland **donate** money to support Trócaire's life-saving work. Trócaire also gets donations from other organisations, including the Irish government. The charity spends around 94 per cent of the money it receives on projects to help poor people. The remaining 6 per cent is spent on fundraising.

In 2018, Irish people donated over €29 million to Trócaire!

Trócaire works with whole communities to help them solve the problems they face. This helps both children and grown-ups. Here's a case study that shows how Trócaire helped one girl and her family.

Kumba's story

In August 2017, a disaster happened on the outskirts of Freetown, the capital of Sierra Leone in West Africa. There was a **devastating** mudslide caused by flooding. It took just four minutes for the mud to **cascade** down the hillside and ruin hundreds of homes.

Seven-year-old Kumba lived there with her family, until the mudslide destroyed their house. They were lucky to be alive – but they still had massive problems. The family had nowhere to live, and Kumba's mam and dad had no way to earn money. All the equipment they needed for their jobs had been destroyed in the mudslide. All Kumba's schoolbooks and her other possessions were gone as well.

Kumba and her family had to go and live in a children's home with many other people who had lost their homes. Trócaire quickly helped them by giving them a pack containing things such as towels, soap, toothbrushes, kettles, plates and other **essential** items so they could keep clean and cook. Trócaire also gave the children school kits containing books, pens and other equipment, so they could get back to their education quickly.

After the disaster, Trócaire carried on helping Kumba's family and others in the same situation, while the people rebuilt their homes and lives.

Conclusion

Life is extremely hard for children living in many parts of the world, especially where there are wars, famines and natural disasters. However, development charities like Trócaire give us a way to help these children and their families by working with local people to solve problems and find a way to build a better life.

A. Comprehension: Fact finding

Answer the questions.

1. What kind of water do all children need?
2. Who helps children when governments can't help them?
3. What are the two main things Trócaire tries to do?
4. How did Trócaire help people in Nepal in 2015?
5. What problems did Kumba and her family have after the mudslide?

Why do you think Trócaire goes on helping after a disaster is over?

B. Comprehension: Read between the lines

Answer the questions.

1. How do you think Kumba felt after the disaster?
2. In your own words, explain why development charities are needed.
3. Why do you think people in Ireland give money to Trócaire?
4. Why was it important for Kumba to get back to school quickly?
5. What might have happened to Kumba without Trócaire?

Which of the things listed on page 116 do you think are most important? Why?

C. Vocabulary

Choose the word or phrase that is nearest in meaning to the underlined word.

1. I like eating candyfloss, but it's not very nutritious.
   a) filling **b)** sensible **c)** edible **d)** healthy
2. Many people believe it's right to fight against injustice.
   a) enemies **b)** unfairness **c)** poverty **d)** helplessness
3. Mam asked me to donate some old toys to the school fair.
   a) deliver **b)** give **c)** sell **d)** show
4. A devastating earthquake destroyed many homes.
   a) disastrous **b)** brief **c)** unexpected **d)** distant
5. Water began to cascade from the sink onto the floor.
   a) travel **b)** pour **c)** rampage **d)** slide
6. It's essential to bring a packed lunch on the trip.
   a) silly **b)** useful **c)** necessary **d)** smart

Use 'essential' and 'nutritious' in a sentence about food.

D. Vocabulary

Choose the most suitable words to complete the paragraph.

developing war-torn access vulnerable aftermath development

In many _______ countries, people are _______ to illness and hunger because of poverty. In _______ areas, the problems can be even worse, and people may not have _______ to food, clean water or safe places to live away from violence. _______ charities work with people in the _______ of wars, famines and natural disasters.

Use words from the box to write about the work that development charities do.

E. Grammar: Conjunctions for cause and effect

Conjunctions like 'because', 'in order to' or 'so' help show how one thing causes another thing to happen. This is called **cause and effect**.

Examples: I was late for school **because** I forgot to set my alarm.
I wanted to buy some crisps, **so** I went to the shop.

The conjunction can come at the start or in the middle of the sentence.

Write the sentences and underline the conjunctions.

1. Aoife rushed home in order to see the new kittens.
2. I'm wearing a thick jumper due to the cold weather.
3. We'll go swimming next week, since the pool's shut today.
4. Because I couldn't find my socks, I missed the bus.
5. It was very noisy downstairs, so I went up to my room.
6. I went to Fergal's house because I like playing with him.

Write the sentences, using the most suitable conjunction to fill each gap.

due to therefore so because in order to

1. I wasn't hungry today _______ I didn't eat my lunch.
2. _______ Mr O'Carroll is sick, there's no PE today.
3. I climbed up the tree _______ get a better view.
4. The match was cancelled _______ the snow.
5. The snowdrops are coming out, _______ it must be nearly spring!

Write a sentence using the conjunction 'so'.

F. Writing skills: Proofreading

When we **proofread**, we check the final draft of our writing to make sure:

- The spellings are correct. ✓
- The punctuation is correct. ✓
- There are no words missing. ✓
- There are no repeated words. ✓

Proofread the text below carefully. Write the paragraph with no mistakes.

Red pandas ar found in the the Eastern Himalayas and South-Western china. Thy are more closely related two raccoons than blakc and white pandas. red pandas live a solitary existence accept during mating season They have loong, bushy tales and raccoon, like features. They are excellent tree climbers And are able to descend threes head furst' There are fewer than 10,000 read pandas in in the wild today

G. Writing genre: Writing a report

Use the KWL chart you made in Unit 10a to write a report about another country.

1. Write your first draft. Remember to include:
   - An introduction saying why you chose this country
   - Three sections on your three different topics
   - A subheading for each section
   - A short conclusion.
2. Reread your first draft.
   - Did you make any mistakes?
   - Could you add any more interesting details?
3. Write the final draft of your report, making any improvements you can. You could add a map, draw illustrations or stick in photos.

You could put all your reports together in a class book about countries around the world!

11a Leaving the Cottage

This classic story is set in Ireland during the Famine (1845–1852).

Many people are dying of hunger and disease. Eily and her brother Michael and sister Peggy are left alone. They wait for days, but their mother does not return. If she doesn't come back soon, the ***landlord****'s assistant Tom Daly has told the children they will have to leave their home. They'll be made go to the* ***workhouse****, where conditions are very* ***harsh*** *and the children will be separated. The thought fills Eily with* ***dread****.*

The next day every hour **dragged**. None of them had the heart for anything. At midday Tom Daly called to the cottage.

'There's no sign, Eily, is there?' he questioned. She shook her head **dumbly**. 'You know what it means. Jer will never stand for three children having a cottage to themselves. You probably haven't enough food for more than a few days anyway, then what's to become of you? The workhouse isn't the worst. These are terrible times – I've seen some awful sights. There will be a crowd on the walk. We'll be leaving tomorrow about mid-morning. Be ready, Eily. I'm sorry, but there's no other way,' he finished.

A. Comprehension: Fact finding

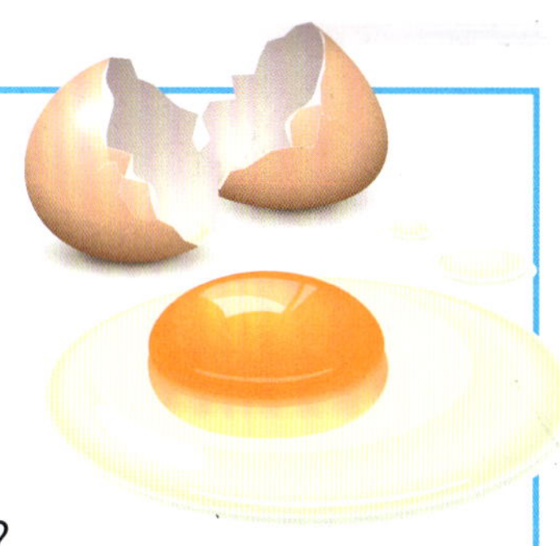

Answer the questions.

1. Where is Gene living at the moment? Why?
2. How did Aunt Joan react to the flying eggs incident?
3. Who is taller, Gene or Wesley?
4. Where does Seamus live?
5. How does Gene feel when Seamus's mother nags him?

Which word does Gene overuse in Diary A? Why do you think he does this?

B. Comprehension: Read between the lines

Answer the questions.

1. Why does Gene say Aunt Joan is a 'dull weight'?
2. Do you feel sorry for Wesley? Why or why not?
3. How does Aunt Joan feel about musicians? How do you know?
4. Would Gene be happier staying with Seamus's family? Why?
5. Why are Diary A and Diary B so different?

Choose five words to describe Gene's character.

C. Vocabulary

Choose the word or phrase that is nearest in meaning to the underlined word.

1. I'm suffocating in this hot room – let's open the window!
   a) unable to breathe **b)** gasping **c)** dead **d)** yawning
2. Jack suddenly had the urge to jump off the wall.
   a) ability **b)** desire **c)** opportunity **d)** courage
3. Miss Murphy droned on and on about the homework.
   a) kept talking **b)** shouted **c)** lied **d)** fussed
4. Mr Marks was cross because of the incident at breaktime.
   a) accident **b)** event **c)** fight **d)** disaster
5. Ciaran went hurtling down the stairs.
   a) limping **b)** hobbling **c)** thumping **d)** flying
6. Rosie deliberately spilled water over Donna's painting.
   a) accidentally **b)** helplessly **c)** purposely **d)** cruelly

Write a sentence to show the meaning of the word 'deliberately'.

D. Vocabulary

Choose the most suitable word to complete each sentence.

1. When Jamie feels sad he _______ around the house. (leaps, sprints, mooches)
2. My woolly scarf is _______ for chilly weather. (intentional, suitable, considerable)
3. If Dad sees us, he's _______ to send us up to bed. (bound, slow, deliberately)
4. Kim has a fashionable _______ of haircut. (trend, style, image)
5. We found the spell book in the magic _______ of the library. (section, partition, condition)
6. A month is _______ longer than a week. (probably, deliberately, certainly)

Write a dictionary definition for one of the underlined words.

E. Grammar: More interesting verbs for 'said'

Writers often replace **'said'** with a **more interesting verb**. This can make your writing more descriptive.

Examples: 'Come here at once!' **thundered** Max.
'I'm sorry,' **whispered** Timothy.
'I won the prize for best singer!' **bragged** Sinéad.

Write the sentence with an interesting verb in each gap.

1. 'You puny weaklings are no match for me!' _______ the supervillain.
2. 'Shhh!' _______ Violet. 'We don't want them to hear us!'
3. 'Don't be so mean!' _______ Riley.
4. 'But I don't want to clean my room!' _______ Niamh.
5. 'You'll never defeat me!' _______ the ogre.

Look at the verbs. Write what each person might have said.

1. '_______' smiled Liam.
2. '_______' cheered Mrs Harris.
3. '_______' sneered the vampire.
4. '_______' giggled Henry.
5. '_______' Mam ordered.
6. '_______' Carmel suggested.

Choose a chapter from a book. List the verbs used instead of 'said'.

F. Writing skills: Varying sentence lengths

Good writing uses a mix of **short** and **long sentences**.

Short sentences can add excitement, suspense and humour.

Example: The door opened. Finn screamed. It was a vampire!

Longer sentences can give important information about the characters or setting.

Example: The vampire wore a long, billowing black cloak with a red silk lining. His face was pale, his teeth were pointy and white and his eyes were red.

Read the text.

Peter and Max scrambled down the long, narrow, thorny path into the woods. Suddenly, Max stopped.

'Are you sure about this?' he asked. 'It's dark in here.'

'Don't be a scaredy cat!' Peter answered. 'This is the fastest way home.'

But Max was silent. His face was pale. His eyes widened. There was something in the bushes ...

Write the next paragraph of the story, using a mix of short and long sentences.

G. Writing genre: Writing a narrative with interesting characters

Use the mind map you made in Unit 11a to write a story with interesting characters.

1. Write your first draft.
    - Use dialogue to show what your characters' personalities are like, what they think of each other and how they feel.
    - Use a mixture of short sentences to add suspense and humour, and long sentences to add detail and explanation.
2. Share your story with a partner and ask for feedback. Do they think it could be improved?
3. Write your final draft, making anyimprovements you can.

12a How to Survive a Wedding

If anyone close to you gets married, you'll know that a wedding can send the grown-ups half-**demented**. Wedding **fever** seems to affect everybody!

It's not just the grown-ups who get involved, either. It's almost **inevitable** you'll get roped in too. You might be invited as a guest, or you might end up with a special job to do, like bridesmaid or usher. Don't panic, though! Just follow these simple instructions, and you'll be fine.

Part 1: Preparing for the big day

You'll need to look your very best ... and that means shopping.

If you're a bridesmaid or usher, you won't get much choice about what you wear. Most likely, everyone will be in matching suits or dresses. You might have to go to a special clothes fitting. If so:

- Try to be patient. Clothes fittings are really boring, but there's no point giving out about it. It just makes the whole thing take even longer.
- Stand still! That's tricky when someone is **prodding** you with pins. But if you wriggle, you'll end up with a suit or dress that's sewn up all wonky!
- Try not to grow between the fitting session and the wedding. Otherwise, you'll be squeezing yourself into your outfit like a sausage in a sausage skin!

If you're a guest, there are loads of **absurd** rules about what you should and shouldn't wear. There are whole *magazines* full of these rules. For example:

- Don't wear white – people might think you're trying to copy the bride.
- Don't wear black – it's not a funeral.
- Don't wear jeans and a T-shirt – you've got to seem like you've made an effort.
- Don't go too bright or showy – you might **detract** attention from the bride.

No wonder the grown-ups get so stressed over their outfits!

Whatever you're wearing on the day, you probably think your wedding clothes are utterly **ridiculous**. But don't worry too much. You'll almost certainly have grown out of them before anyone can make you wear them again.

Part 2: The morning of the wedding

Here are some tips to help you get through the pre-wedding **chaos**.

- Start off with a clean face and tidy hair. They might not last long, but at least you can say you tried.
- Put on your wedding outfit. Brace yourself for relatives to cry when they see you looking so smart and grown-up. Try not to roll your eyes or pull funny faces when they can't resist sneaking a photo!
- Pack a survival kit for the big day. You'll need:
  - Snacks (in case you don't like the food)
  - Water (weddings are thirsty work)
  - A game or book (let's face it, it could be a *long* day)
  - Tissues (because no matter what, somebody will cry)
  - Camera or phone (so you can take lots of embarrassing pictures of your relatives).

Part 3: The ceremony

If you're a bridesmaid or usher:

- Remember your part! But don't worry, someone will remind you what to do if you forget.
- If in doubt, look out for the bride and groom and do what they tell you.
- Smile! It'll make everyone feel **perkier** (even you!).

If you're a guest:

- Try not to fall asleep during the **ceremony**. Or at least, if you do, try not to snore.
- Don't giggle at the mushy readings or poems.
- Don't play games on your phone during the ceremony – and no selfies, either!

Part 4: The reception

This bit is meant to be fun! In reality, the wedding reception can be a little bit on the dull side. Follow our tips, though, and you should get through it just fine.

Food

With a bit of luck there'll be something you like on the menu. But if not:

- Hide what you don't like under a handy lettuce leaf.
- Steal the bits you do like from your parents' plates.
- Max out on bread rolls.
- Be glad you packed some emergency snacks!

Dancing

This can go on for hours! Here are some tips to help you avoid boredom on the dance floor.

- Find a job to do. Maybe you can help clear tables, or organise a game for the younger children.
- Get together with the other kids. There's usually someone who's up for some fun. You could share any games or activities you've brought.
- **Appoint** yourself (un)official photographer. You're bound to get some interesting shots that the main wedding photographer will miss! You might even get some embarrassing photos of your parents on the dance floor, which you can use to blackmail them later ...

Part 5: When it's all over

Congratulations! You've survived a wedding!

Remember to tell the bride and groom what a lovely time you had. Don't mention the boring or stressful bits! One nice way to say thank you is by using all your photos to make a fun scrapbook for the bride and groom. Then you can start getting ready for the next wedding!

A. Comprehension: Fact finding

Answer the questions.

1. What job might a girl or boy have at a wedding?
2. Why shouldn't you wear black to a wedding?
3. Why is it a good idea to bring snacks?
4. List two ways you could amuse yourself during the dancing.
5. Name one thing you could do with your photos afterwards.

Which section do you think is most useful? Why?

B. Comprehension: Read between the lines

Answer the questions.

1. Who is the audience for this text? How do you know?
2. Which survival item do you think is most important? Why?
3. Say in your own words why the ceremony might make you giggle.
4. What kind of food do you think might be served at a wedding?
5. Does the text make you want to go to a wedding? Why or why not?

How is this different from most procedures? How is it the same?

C. Vocabulary

Choose the word or phrase that is nearest in meaning to the underlined word.

1. The witch's demented laughter echoed around the cave.
   a) quiet **b)** amused **c)** mad **d)** exhausted
2. There was an inevitable delay before the bus left.
   a) unavoidable **b)** boring **c)** unpleasant **d)** long
3. Alana kept prodding the cake with her fork.
   a) moving **b)** poking **c)** eating **d)** mixing
4. My costume for the play was absurd.
   a) daft **b)** elaborate **c)** too small **d)** glamorous
5. Nothing could detract from the fun of the party.
   a) come **b)** exclude **c)** distract **d)** take away
6. It was chaos when a cat got loose at the dog show.
   a) funny **b)** interesting **c)** mayhem **d)** terrible

Write a sentence describing a scene of chaos.

D. Vocabulary

Choose the most suitable word to complete each sentence.

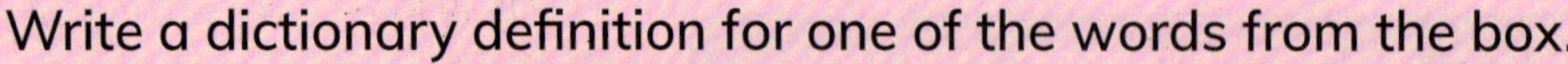

fever ridiculous perkier ceremony appointed

1. Dad ______ himself the official barbecue chef.
2. I looked ______ in my wedding outfit.
3. I was tired this morning, but after lunch I felt ______.
4. Jamie was ill with a ______ and had a high temperature.
5. I promised I would behave during the wedding ______.

Write a dictionary definition for one of the words from the box.

E. Grammar: Adjectives and comparative adjectives

Adjectives are describing words. Adjectives describe **nouns**.

Examples: The bride wore a **beautiful white** dress. The wedding was **fun**.

Write the paragraph. Choose adjectives to fill the blanks.

Yesterday was Clodagh's birthday. First we saw a ______ movie in the cinema. We ate lots of ______ popcorn and ______ ice cream. After that, we played some ______ games in Clodagh's house and had ______ pizza for dinner. It was a ______ success. Clodagh was very ______.

Comparative adjectives compare two people or things.

For most adjectives, add -er to make it a comparative. **Example:** tall**er**.

For adjectives ending in -y, remove the y and add -ier. **Example:** happ**ier**.

Write the comparative of each adjective.

young clean heavy bright

Write the sentences, changing the words in brackets to comparative adjectives.

1. The sloth was slow but the snail was (slow).
2. Kiara is (old) than Megan.
3. The movie was much (funny) than I expected.
4. A mouse is (small) than an elephant.

Write about someone you admire, using comparative adjectives.

F. Writing skills: Features of a procedure

Most **procedures**:

- Have a title that tells what the aim is. **Example:** How to play Snap
- List any materials and equipment needed
- Use bossy verbs. **Examples:** make, put
- Tell the reader what to do in order
- Have numbered steps
- Finish with an evaluation.

Rewrite this procedure, following the rules above.

Making a smoothie

The first thing you need to do is get a ripe banana and peel it. Now chop the banana up and put it in your electric mixer. If you've got a handful of blueberries in the fruit bowl, those would be nice too. Add some ice cubes and switch the mixer on. Oh! I forgot to say, you need to add a cup of milk too, before you mix it. The fruit, milk and ice will get all mixed up together and turn smooth and creamy. Then you can drink it. But you need to pour it into a glass before you do that. See what you think of your smoothie – does it taste OK?

G. Writing genre: Planning a procedure

Plan a procedure on how to make something for a party.

1. Decide what your instructions will be for. Choose one of the suggestions below, or come up with your own idea. It should be fun, but quite simple to make.

a party hat | a table decoration | a party food | something to drink

2. Write a list of the materials and equipment needed.
3. Make notes about what you have to do at each step.
4. Decide how you will evaluate it.

12b Crafty Table Decorations

If someone you know is getting married or having a party, it's good to lend a hand with the **preparations**. It's even better if you can use your **crafting** skills to make something really special! Here are two ideas for **unique** table decorations you could make as a **thoughtful** gift for any special occasion.

Origami swans

These clever origami swans will look very stylish, swimming **serenely** down the centre of the party tables.

What you need

Squares of paper. You could use proper origami paper. Or you could cut squares from large sheets of colourful craft paper. Choose colours that will match the colour **scheme** of the event. You could even use pages from newspapers or magazines, for a **distinctive** look!

What to do

1. Take a square of paper and fold it in half diagonally. Then unfold it.

2. Fold the left and right edges of the paper to meet the crease in the centre.

3. Turn the paper over and do the same thing again. Fold in the left and right edges to meet the central crease.

4. Now fold the sharp pointy end back so that it touches the other end.

5. Fold the sharp point back no more than one-third of the way along.

6. Fold the model in half down the centre crease.

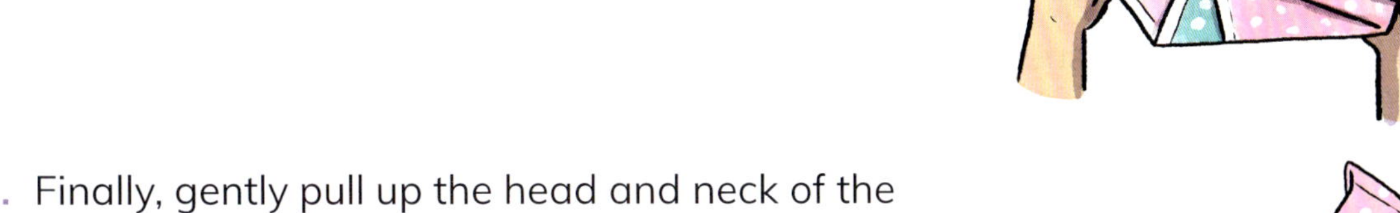

7. Finally, gently pull up the head and neck of the swan. You may need to refold the crease at the base of the neck so that it stands up properly.

Your swan table decoration is finished! Now make some more so it has some friends to swim with.

Funky tealight holders

You can make these creative tealight holders any colour you like. They will look particularly nice if they match other colours used in the event.

What you need

Materials:

- Clear glass tealight holders, glasses or small bowls
- Coloured tissue paper
- PVA glue or other **adhesive** that dries clear
- Tealights or small candles

Equipment:

- Scissors
- Brush

Safety tip

If you're using glasses or bowls instead of tealight holders, make sure they are suitable for holding a lit candle. Ask a grown-up to help you check.

D. Vocabulary

Choose the most suitable words to complete the paragraph.

random preparations thoughtful overlapping scheme effects

It was _______ of Will and Ciara to help with the _______ for the party. The theme was 'under the sea'. They crafted a giant fish out of old milk cartons, with _______ scales made from recycled sweet wrappers, stuck on at _______. They got some great _______ using blue and green sweet wrappers that complemented the colour _______ for the party.

Write a sentence describing an animal, using 'distinctive'.

E. Grammar: Choosing more interesting adjectives

Some adjectives are overused.

Examples: a **nice** sandwich, a **good** story.

Choosing more **interesting, precise adjectives** can improve your writing.

Examples: a **scrumptious** sandwich, a **riveting** story.

Write the sentences with more interesting adjectives.

1. We had a nice time at Jackson's party.
2. Emily is good at scoring goals.
3. There was a pretty bunch of flowers on the table.
4. A small sparrow was hopping about by my feet.
5. Amy had a sad look on her face.
6. The big, scary giant roared at us.

Write the sentences with interesting adjectives in the gaps.

1. We climbed up the _______ hill to the _______ tower.
2. Ella has a _______ dog called Cosmo.
3. Abby put on a _______ dress. She looked _______.
4. The sea was _______ during the storm.
5. There was a _______ cake, and it looked _______.
6. The _______ goblin gave a _______ snarl.

Write lists of adjectives you could use instead of 'big' and 'small'.

F. Writing skills: Helpful illustrations

Instructions often include **illustrations**. These can:

- Break up complicated instructions into clear steps
- Show the reader what the thing they're making looks like at each stage
- Help the reader to check they've understood the written instructions.

These illustrations show the steps in making hot chocolate.
Write an instruction to go with each illustration.

G. Writing genre: Writing a procedure

Use the notes you made in Unit 12a to write a procedure on how to make something for a party.

1. Write your first draft. Remember to:
   - Say what the aim of the procedure is
   - List the equipment and materials needed
   - Use bossy verbs such as 'cut' and 'make'
   - Write the steps in order
   - Add illustrations where they are helpful
   - Finish with an evaluation.
2. Swap procedures with a partner. If you can, try following their instructions. Did they work? Suggest improvements your partner could make.
3. Write your final draft, making any improvements you can.

You could make a class party-planning book with all your instructions in it!

13a How are Comic Books Made?

Do you like reading comics or comic-style books? Perhaps you've even had a go at writing a comic strip story yourself? Here's how a writer called Declan and an artist called Lucy made a comic about a new superhero, Captain Rabbit.

Early ideas

First, Lucy and Declan think and talk about Captain Rabbit and his character. What will he be like? What kinds of adventures will he have? Then Declan starts to write the **script** of the first story. To begin with, he just sums up the main things that will happen using short sentences. These sentences are called beats. Beats are a good way to start, because they help Declan and Lucy to imagine the story. They are also quick to write and easy to change.

Captain Rabbit: The First Adventure

Beat 1: Captain Rabbit is **bounding** across the rooftops in the city.

Beat 2: He sees a bank robbery.

Beat 3: He bounces down to stop the robbers.

Beat 4: The robbers try to get away, but Captain Rabbit throws his special attack-carrots.

Beat 5: The attack-carrots explode and nets shoot out. The robbers are caught.

Meanwhile, Lucy has been trying to draw Captain Rabbit. She's not **satisfied** with her first set of **designs**. They make Captain Rabbit look a bit too tough and **sinister**!

Then she has the idea of making him look a bit daft and clumsy. She does a quick sketch, and shows Declan. He likes it too! Captain Rabbit looks like a much more **humorous** character now!

The script

Now Declan turns the beats into a script. He imagines the story as panels in the comic. He describes the picture for each panel, as well as all the words that will appear in speech bubbles and **caption** boxes.

A panel is one of the frames that make up a comic strip. They're usually square or rectangular, but they can be other shapes too.

The words in a comic strip can go in caption boxes, speech bubbles or thought bubbles. Sometimes there are special effects too, like 'Aaargh!' and 'Splat!'

Here is Declan's script for the first two panels.

Panel 1: View of the city at night. The rooftops are shown in **silhouette** against a big full moon. Captain Rabbit is in the distance, leaping across the rooftops. At this point he looks quite impressive, like a 'proper' superhero.

CAPTION: While the city sleeps, someone is keeping watch. Someone who never **ceases** in his fight against evil. That someone is ...

Panel 2: Zoom in on Captain Rabbit's face. Now we can see he looks quite harmless, with big teeth and googly eyes. He has long rabbit ears – one is sticking up and the other is flopping down.

CAPTION: ... Captain Rabbit!

THOUGHT BUBBLE FROM Captain Rabbit: There are burglars about – I'd better get hopping!

Lucy and Declan **discuss** the script. Lucy thinks at first that we should see Captain Rabbit from above, but decides in the end that a close-up focus on the robbers will be more dramatic. Declan changes the script as their ideas change. It's much quicker to change things now than it will be when Lucy's done the artwork!

The artwork

When the script for the first story is finished, Lucy has a lot of drawing to do. She draws using a computer. She does all the **outlines** of the drawings first – this is called pencilling. When she is happy with them, she colours them in. This stage is known as inking. Finally, she adds the words in the captions and speech bubbles. When she's finished, all the artwork and text for the first story is in a computer file.

In the days before computers, a team of artists would draw on large sheets of thick paper. First, a penciller would do the outlines, then an inker would colour them in, and then a letterer would add the words. The different artists **collaborated** as a team (especially if a lot of stories had to be made quickly). Finally, the art would be photographed, and the photograph was then used by the printer to make printed comics.

Publishing

Lucy and Declan send their story to Andy Miller, who publishes a comic. Andy reads the story, and he likes it. He offers to publish some Captain Rabbit stories in his comic. He suggests a few changes to the text and the artwork of the first story.

Finally, when Lucy has made the changes, Andy sends all the computer files for the comic to a printing company. They use the files to print lots of paper copies of the comic, which go to the shops for people to buy.

Nowadays, some comics aren't published on paper – they appear on websites instead.

A. Comprehension: Fact finding

Answer the questions.

1. What is the name of the artist of the comic strip?
2. How do beats help to plan a comic story?
3. What was wrong with the first drawings of Captain Rabbit?
4. What shapes are comic strip frames usually?
5. What is the 'colouring in' stage of drawing a comic called?

Do you prefer the first sketch of Captain Rabbit or the final one? Why?

B. Comprehension: Read between the lines

Answer the questions.

1. How do Lucy and Declan start planning the comic?
2. Why should you get the story right before doing the artwork?
3. Why do Lucy and Declan need Andy?
4. Do you think it's easier to make comics now than it was in the past? Why?
5. Who contributes most to the comic – Lucy, Declan or both? Why?

Do you think creating a comic requires a lot of skill? Why or why not?

C. Vocabulary

Choose the word or phrase that is nearest in meaning to the underlined word.

1. The dog went <u>bounding</u> across the field.
   a) trotting **b)** leaping **c)** flying **d)** zigzagging
2. Lucy felt <u>satisfied</u> with her picture.
   a) annoyed **b)** unhappy **c)** pleased **d)** disappointed
3. The puppy looked <u>humorous</u> with his long ears flapping.
   a) sinister **b)** unusual **c)** clumsy **d)** funny
4. My teacher called my parents to <u>discuss</u> my homework.
   a) talk about **b)** think about **c)** complain about **d)** ask about
5. Grandad never <u>ceases</u> working on his garden.
   a) stops **b)** dislikes **c)** begins **d)** regrets
6. The two authors <u>collaborated</u> on a book.
   a) worked together **b)** disagreed **c)** agreed **d)** decided

Find dictionary definitions for 'satisfied' and 'humorous'.

D. Vocabulary

Choose the most suitable words to complete the paragraph.

designs silhouette captions sinister script outlines

The artist looked at the _______ that the writer had prepared. The main character was a _______ villain. The artist decided to show him first as a _______ with strong, bold _______ against the white of the moon. The artist was pleased with her _______ for the villain. The writer wrote some good _______ to go with the panels.

Write about a superhero or villain using 'sinister' or 'humorous'.

E. Grammar: Subject-verb agreement

The **subject** of a sentence is the main person or thing the sentence is about.
The subject should always **agree** with the **verb**.
If the subject is singular, then the verb should also be singular.
Example: The **superhero is** flying.
If the subject is plural, then the verb should also be plural.
Example: The **superheroes are** flying.

Write the sentences. Choose the correct verbs to fill the blanks.

1. We _______ eating cake. (is, are)
2. The girls _______ excited. (was, were)
3. Matthew _______ tired. (is, are)
4. Aoife _______ next door. (live, lives)
5. We _______ lunch at 12. (has, have)
6. They _______ ice cream. (love, loves)

Write the sentences, correcting the verb so it agrees with the subject.

1. My brother sleep in the top bunk.
2. They always eats porridge for breakfast.
3. Sarah enjoy playing football.
4. The children works very hard.
5. The baby are asleep.

Rewrite this sentence, changing the subject to 'she':
I walk to school.

F. Writing skills: Cause and effect

Sometimes, one event can make another happen. The **cause** is why the event happened and the **effect** is what happened.

Explanation texts often use conjunctions such as 'because', 'so', 'due to' and 'therefore' to link cause and effect.

Examples: Astronauts float in space **because** they do not have enough gravity pulling on them.

Lucy wasn't happy with her design, **so** she changed it.

Decide which cause goes with which effect and write the sentences correctly in your copy. (**Hint:** sometimes the effect is written first.)

Cause	Effect
Anna studied hard for the test.	so we brought her to the vet.
because it is faster.	The 3 p.m. train is delayed
Our cat Cindy was sick,	I prefer cycling to walking
due to wet leaves on the track.	Therefore, she got good marks.

Write effects for these causes.

1. I was hungry, so ...
2. Since it was snowing, ...
3. Because of the amount of homework I had ...
4. I love spending time outdoors. Therefore ...

G. Writing genre: Planning an explanation text

Plan an explanation

1. First, choose one of these titles:
   - ★ Why do we yawn?
   - ★ Why do we sneeze?
   - ★ Why do we dream?
   - ★ Why do we get hiccups?
2. Use books and the internet to research the answer to your question.
3. Organise your information into sections. Write a subheading for each section.
4. The audience for your explanation is other children in your class. Think about how you can you make your explanation appealing to them.

13b Why Do We laugh?

Did you hear the one about the scientist who tried to find out why people laugh? She got so many books about laughter that her bookcase fell down. She only had her shelf to blame.

OK, maybe that wasn't very funny! But it's true that scientists have spent a lot of time trying to work out why we laugh. Let's take a look at some common questions about laughing.

Why do people laugh in groups?

A scientist called Robert Provine and his **assistants** watched people to find out when they laughed. They found that people mostly laughed when they were talking to each other. Usually it wasn't when someone had told a **deliberate** joke.

Robert Provine thought this showed that laughing was about showing playfulness. When you laugh, you show that you like the people around you and want to be part of their group. That also explains why it feels bad to be laughed at if you didn't mean to be funny. The people who are laughing are showing that they are all in the same group, but you are not.

Did I have to learn how to laugh?

It seems that people are born knowing how to laugh. Babies can laugh when they are about four months old – that's long before they can talk or understand what is said to them. People who are born both blind and deaf can laugh. This shows that you don't need to learn how to laugh by watching or listening to other people.

Do any animals laugh?

Apes are the animals most like humans. They also do something a bit like laughing. Chimps make an open-mouthed **expression** with their bottom teeth showing, called a 'play face'. When they are doing this, chimps often pant and make a 'ha ha' sound. They often make a play face when playing chasing games or play-fighting.

So a play face seems to show the chimp understands this is for fun, rather than real fighting. The fact that chimps also laugh (in a way) might tell us that laughing **evolved** before modern people did.

Why does tickling make me laugh?

Scientists found that tickling **activates** part of the brain that decides what to do when you're in danger. Tickling also activates part of the brain that is about nice feelings. So it seems that people laugh when their brains realise that the tickling is a sort of play attack. They are showing that they know the 'attack' isn't dangerous. That might explain why you can sometimes make someone laugh just by **threatening** to tickle them.

Being tickled by something unexpected – like a spider landing on your arm – doesn't make you laugh, because that isn't a game. And you can't make yourself laugh by tickling yourself, because you know the tickle is coming.

Why do I sometimes cry when I laugh?

Crying and laughing are both things we do when we're feeling **emotional**. Scientists think laughter and tears are both ways to **relieve** stress. So maybe they can get a bit mixed up. Laughing also puts **pressure** on your tear ducts, which can make tears come out. Also, people who are laughing pant a lot, and could breathe in dust or pollen from the air, making their eyes water.

Why can't I stop laughing?

Because laughing is to do with being emotional, it's very difficult to stop laughing right away when you want to. In fact, knowing that you really shouldn't be laughing can make it harder to stop! But people normally do stop laughing before long.

Sometimes we say laughter is **contagious**, meaning it spreads from one person to another like a disease. Usually this is just a saying, but in 1962 there was an odd outbreak of what was called '*omuneepo*' (which means 'laughing disease'). It happened in Tanzania in Africa. Three girls at a boarding school started laughing, and couldn't stop. Other students started laughing too. So many students couldn't stop laughing that the school had to close. Most people laughed for a few hours or less, but one girl said she kept laughing for 16 days. Doctors noticed that the school where *omuneepo* started was very strict and overcrowded. They thought these bad **conditions** made the girls feel very stressed, and the laughing was a sort of **protest**.

Conclusion

Laughing is a human instinct that we share with some other animals. People sometimes laugh when they are upset, but usually it is a signal to other people that we're having fun.

A. Comprehension: Fact finding

Answer the questions.

1. Name a scientist who has studied laughter.
2. At what age do people usually start laughing?
3. Which animals are most like humans?
4. What is a 'play face'?
5. Where and when did a case of *omuneepo* happen?

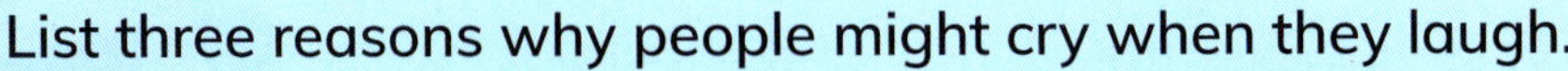

List three reasons why people might cry when they laugh.

B. Comprehension: Read between the lines

Answer the questions.

1. Why do you think this explanation starts with a joke?
2. What do you notice about the headings in this text?
3. Give three reasons why people laugh.
4. Do you think this is a good explanation? Why or why not?
5. Which fact did you find most surprising? Why?

Write about a time you couldn't stop laughing.

C. Vocabulary

Choose the word or phrase that is nearest in meaning to the underlined word.

1. The scientist had three lab assistants.
   a) volunteers **b)** teachers **c)** children **d)** helpers
2. Humans and apes evolved from the same ancestor.
   a) slowly developed **b)** were removed **c)** improved **d)** were born
3. The alarm activates if the door is opened.
   a) starts **b)** improves **c)** stops **d)** breaks
4. Dad took some medicine to relieve his headache.
   a) forget **b)** soothe **c)** strengthen **d)** shorten
5. Measles is a rare disease these days, but it's very contagious.
   a) painful **b)** infectious **c)** uncommon **d)** easily cured
6. The people protested about their bad treatment.
   a) laughed **b)** wailed **c)** disagreed **d)** complained

Write a dictionary definition for one of the underlined words.

D. Vocabulary

Choose the most suitable word to complete each sentence.

1. Mam was cross because Danny told a _______ lie. (contagious, deliberate, threatening)
2. The _______ on Dad's face was funny. (pressure, expression, conditions)
3. The storm clouds were _______ rain. (confusing, protesting, threatening)
4. People often cry when they are feeling _______. (threatening, hopeful, emotional)
5. We needed to let off steam after the _______ of the tests. (emotion, pressure, conditions)
6. The _______ in the prison were very bad. (pressures, protests, conditions)

Write a sentence about laughing, using one of the words you chose.

E. Grammar: Prepositions – time, place and direction

Prepositions tell us about the time, place or direction of movement of a person or thing.

Draw the table below. Put the prepositions from the boxes in the correct columns. Some prepositions belong in more than one column.

in | on | to | through | beside | at | from | during | towards

Time	Place	Direction
until	on top of	up

Write the sentences, filling each gap with a preposition from the box.

while on past towards through during

1. We tiptoed _______ the silent forest.
2. I ate my lunch _______ reading my comic.
3. The ball shot _______ the goalkeeper.
4. I found my sunglasses _______ the table.
5. I couldn't help laughing _______ the play.
6. Cara walked _______ the sunlit stream.

Write two sentences using the prepositions 'above' and 'below'.

F. Writing skills: Subheadings and paragraphs

Explanation texts are usually divided up into clear sections with:

- **Subheadings** to show what the topic of each section is
- **Paragraphs** to divide up information within the sections.

Start a new section for each new topic, and a new paragraph when there is a change of **subject**, **time** or **place**.

Read this section from an explanation text. Rewrite it, adding:

- A subheading that says what the section is about
- A paragraph break when there is a change in subject, time or place.

Most scientists agree that crying can be a way of asking for help from other people. It is a sign that something is wrong. So if you cry when you're sad, it's a way of saying, 'Come and help me.' Lots of animals make loud sounds when they are upset – but humans are among the few animals that produce tears. One theory to explain why we cry quietly rather than yelling loudly is that loud noises can be dangerous. Yelling could attract predators, as well as your mam! So there's an advantage in sending a signal for help *quietly*.

G. Writing genre: Writing an explanation text

Use the plan you made in Unit 13a to write an explanation text.

1. Write your first draft. Remember to:
    - Use subheadings.
    - Include all the information your readers will need to understand your topic.
    - Start a new paragraph whenever the subject, time or place you are writing about changes.
2. Ask a partner to read your explanation and give you feedback. Was it clear and easy to understand?
3. Check your work carefully and correct any mistakes before writing your final draft. Make any improvements you can.

14a Miss Trunchbull

Before the first week of term was up, **awesome** tales about the Headmistress, Miss Trunchbull, began to filter through to the newcomers. Matilda and Lavender, standing in a corner of the playground during morning-break on the third day, were approached by a **rugged** ten-year-old with a boil on her nose, called Hortensia. 'New scum, I suppose,' Hortensia said to them, looking down from her great height. She was eating from an extra-large bag of potato crisps and digging the stuff out in handfuls. 'Welcome to borstal,' she added, spraying bits of crisp out of her mouth like snowflakes.

The two tiny ones, **confronted** by this giant, kept a **watchful** silence.

'Have you met the Trunchbull yet?' Hortensia asked.

'We've seen her at prayers,' Lavender said, 'but we haven't met her.'

'You've got a treat coming to you,' Hortensia said. 'She hates very small children. She therefore **loathes** the bottom class and everyone in it. She thinks five-year-olds are grubs that haven't yet hatched out.' In went another fistful of crisps and when she spoke again, out sprayed the crumbs. 'If you survive your first year you may just manage to live through the rest of your time here. But many don't survive. They get carried out on stretchers screaming. I've seen it often.'

Hortensia paused to **observe** the effect these remarks were having on the two titchy ones. Not very much. They seemed pretty cool. So the large one decided to **regale** them with further information.

'I suppose you know the Trunchbull has a lock-up cupboard in her private quarters called The Chokey? Have you heard about The Chokey?'

Matilda and Lavender shook their heads and continued to gaze up at the giant. Being very small, they were **inclined** to **mistrust** any creature that was larger than they were, especially senior girls.

'The Chokey,' Hortensia went on, 'is a very tall but very narrow cupboard. The floor is only ten inches square so you can't sit down or squat in it. You have to stand. And three of the walls are made of cement with bits of broken glass sticking out all over, so you can't lean against them. You have to stand more or less at attention all the time when you get locked up in there. It's terrible.'

'Can't you lean against the door?' Matilda asked.

'Don't be daft,' Hortensia said. 'The door's got thousands of sharp spiky nails sticking out of it. They've been hammered through from the outside, probably by the Trunchbull herself.'

'Have you ever been in there?' Lavender asked.

'My first term I was in there six times,' Hortensia said. 'Twice for a whole day and the other times for two hours each. But two hours is quite bad enough. It's pitch dark and you have to stand up dead straight and if you wobble at all you get spiked either by the glass on the walls or the nails on the door.'

'Why were you put in?' Matilda asked. 'What had you done?'

'The first time,' Hortensia said, 'I poured half a tin of Golden Syrup on to the seat of the chair the Trunchbull was going to sit on at prayers. It was wonderful. When she lowered herself into the chair, there was a loud squelching noise similar to that made by a hippopotamus when lowering its foot into the mud on the banks of the Limpopo River. But you're too small and stupid to have read the *Just So Stories*, aren't you?'

'I've read them,' Matilda said.

'You're a liar,' Hortensia said **amiably**. 'You can't even read yet. But no matter. So when the Trunchbull sat down on the Golden Syrup, the squelch was beautiful. And when she jumped up again, the chair sort of stuck to the seat of those awful green breeches she wears and came up with her for a few seconds until the thick syrup slowly came unstuck. Then she **clasped** her hands to the seat of her breeches and both hands got covered in the muck. You should have heard her bellow.'

'But how did she know it was you?' Lavender asked.

'A little squirt called Ollie Bogwhistle sneaked on me,' Hortensia said. 'I knocked his front teeth out.'

'And the Trunchbull put you in The Chokey for a whole day?' Matilda asked, gulping.

'All day long,' Hortensia said. 'I was off my rocker when she let me out. I was **babbling** like an idiot.'

Extract from Matilda *by Roald Dahl, published by Penguin Books Ltd.*

A. Comprehension: Fact finding

Answer the questions.

1. Where is Matilda at the start of the story?
2. What is Hortensia eating?
3. What does Miss Trunchbull think of small children?
4. Why couldn't you lean against the door of The Chokey?
5. Why did Hortensia first get sent to The Chokey?

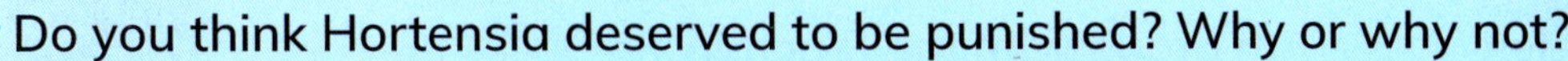

Do you think Hortensia deserved to be punished? Why or why not?

B. Comprehension: Read between the lines

Answer the questions.

1. What does, 'You've got a treat coming to you' *really* mean?
2. Describe The Chokey in your own words.
3. Why does Hortensia tell Matilda and Lavender about The Chokey?
4. Choose five words that describe Hortensia's personality.
5. Would you like to attend Matilda's school? Why or why not?

Which part of the extract do you think is funniest? Why?

C. Vocabulary

Choose the word or phrase that is nearest in meaning to the underlined word.

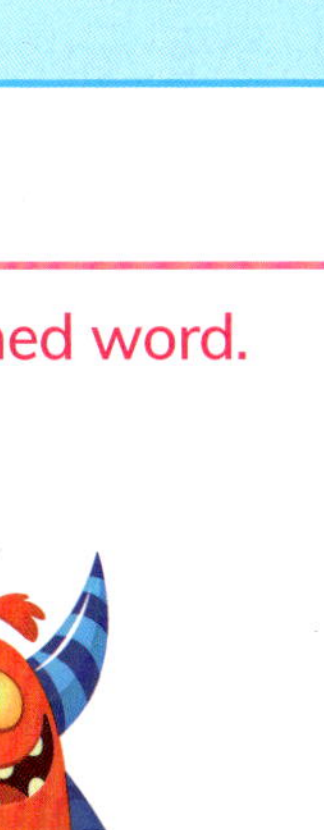

1. Granny told us some <u>awesome</u> stories about her childhood.
   a) amazing **b)** terrifying **c)** funny **d)** nice
2. The <u>rugged</u> explorer hacked through the jungle.
   a) lonely **b)** exhausted **c)** ragged **d)** tough
3. Dad kept a <u>watchful</u> eye on the toddlers.
   a) careless **b)** careful **c)** helpful **d)** critical
4. Our cat Jasper <u>loathes</u> getting wet.
   a) loves **b)** hates **c)** puts up with **d)** enjoys
5. The monster smiled <u>amiably</u>.
   a) in a friendly way **b)** in a sinister way **c)** helpfully **d)** sleepily
6. 'B-but I didn't mean to!' Jen <u>babbled</u> nervously.
   a) shouted **b)** said **c)** mumbled **d)** cried

Look up 'babble' in a dictionary. Write down all the definitions.

D. Vocabulary

Choose the most suitable word to complete each sentence.

confronted regale inclined mistrust clasped observe

1. Our dog has a deep _______ of strangers.
2. 'Did you do this?' Dad _______ me, pointing to the broken vase.
3. From high in the tree, I could _______ everyone below.
4. Grandad began to _______ us with one of his long, boring stories.
5. Nobody felt _______ to argue with the teacher.
6. Grace _______ her hands together anxiously.

Write a sentence about an argument using the word 'confronted'.

E. Grammar: Adverbs (part 1)

Adverbs give us more information about verbs. They usually end in *-ly*.
Examples: Kate shouted **loudly**. The birds sang **sweetly**.

Write the sentences. Circle the verbs and underline the adverbs.

1. We walked quickly to school.
2. Grainne and Pete ran downstairs happily.
3. The performing hippos danced gracefully.
4. 'No!' snapped Emily rudely.
5. The moon was shining brightly on the sea.

Write the sentences, filling each gap with an appropriate adverb.

1. 'Hi, James!' said Eamon _______.
2. The goblins tiptoed _______ down the corridor.
3. The football fans cheered _______.
4. Jane yawned _______.
5. Mam _______ rocked the baby in her arms.
6. The bats flew _______ around the castle.

Write six adverbs that could be used with 'said'.

F. Writing skills: Describing places

Stories often include interesting **descriptions of places**. These include:

- Descriptive words such as adverbs and adjectives
- Interesting details to help readers picture the place.

Example:

adjective

The **haunted** house was full of **dusty** furniture and ghosts that wailed **mournfully** in the night.

adverb

Write the sentences, adding descriptive adjectives and adverbs to make them more interesting.

1. The sun shone on a field full of flowers and grass.
2. Alex walked along the beach, watching the waves.
3. There were lots of people rushing around in the airport.
4. I walked into the classroom, which was full of children.

Write two sentences about a zoo. Include interesting details about the sights, sounds and smells.

G. Writing genre: Planning a fantasy narrative

Plan a fantasy story set in an imaginary place.

1. Think about the sort of place you'd like to set your story in. It could be:
   - ★ An alien planet
   - ★ A spooky wood
   - ★ A deserted village
   - ★ A monster's cave
   - ★ Somewhere else.

2. Make a sensory mind map. Include:
   - What you can **see** when you're there
   - What sounds you can **hear** there
   - What you can **smell** and **taste** when you're there
   - How you **feel** when you're there.
3. List some interesting adjectives and adverbs that will help you describe your chosen place.

14b Babe the Blue Ox

Paul Bunyan is a character in many traditional American stories. He's a giant-sized lumberjack. A lot of odd things seem to happen to him!

Listen up, now! I've got a story for you about my friend Paul Bunyan, and every word of it is true.

Imagine the tallest person you've ever seen. Now picture another person the same size standing on their shoulders. And then a third person just as gigantic standing on *their* shoulders. Well, that's about the size of Paul Bunyan. He's the **mightiest**, strongest and best lumberjack in all of America! He's so enormous he can chop down a whole stand of pine trees with one swishing swing of his axe. Even his teeth are big! When he wants to get them clean, he has to use a pine **sapling** as a toothpick.

When Paul was born, he was the biggest baby the world had ever seen. It took five super-sized storks 12 hours to deliver him to his parents! When he opened his mouth for his first cry, it boomed so loudly that it emptied a whole pond full of frogs. They all **tumbled** off into the undergrowth, trying to cover their ears with their feet as they hopped.

Paul started big, and he just kept on getting bigger. Within a week he had to wear his father's clothes. Soon, however, even these were too tiny for him. His mother had to use telegraph poles to knit him a jacket that would fit. Normal buttons were no use, so she used cartwheels instead. Paul's parents couldn't find a cradle big enough for him to sleep in – so they made a gigantic raft and set him to sleep on the sea. When he turned in his sleep, he made a tidal wave that **capsized** ships for miles around.

When Paul got a little older, his father decided it was time for him to learn to be a lumberjack. He gave Paul his own giant-sized axe and saw, and Paul played with these the way other children played with toys. Soon, Paul was master of the lumberjacking trade. It would take 30 grown men two days to cut down the number of trees Paul **felled** in 10 minutes.

Paul was happy being a lumberjack, but like all children, he wanted a friend to play with. Unfortunately for Paul, he was so much huger than the other children that he couldn't join in their games. It was a lonely life for Paul, until one icy-cold winter things changed for the better.

The year Paul turned ten, it was so cold that all the spiders turned into icicles. The fish swam round and round in circles to keep warm, and even the snow turned blue. The nights were so **glacial** that all the spoken words froze solid. You had to wait till the morning to find out what everyone was saying the night before.

That winter, the blue snow **drifted** so deep that it came all the way up to Paul's knees! It didn't stop him going out to play in the woods, though. He'd been wading through the snow for about half an hour when he heard a most peculiar noise. It was a bit like a snort, and a bit like a bleat – a blort, perhaps, or a sneat. Paul followed the noise. It came from a titchy, little, baby blue ox. He was jumping about in the snow, blorting with fury because he was too **minute** to see over the massive snowdrifts.

Well, Paul couldn't help laughing. He was impressed by the tiny **mite**'s bravery. So he slipped the little blue ox inside his jacket and took him home. He soon had that **shivery** little creature warmed up in front of the fire. Even when he was **toasty** warm, though, that little ox stayed as blue as the snow he'd been found in. So Paul called him Babe the Blue Ox.

Babe quickly grew to be almost as big as Paul. People used to say that if you just stood still and watched, you'd see Babe growing in front of your eyes. He grew so big that the distance between his tail tip and his ears was more than a day's flight for a fit young eagle. You can imagine it took a lot of food to keep Babe going. His mid-morning snack was a hundred bales of hay, and then he still had room for a tonne of corn-cobs for lunch.

Paul and Babe soon became great friends. They laughed at the same jokes, enjoyed the same games and passed many happy hours just spending time together. They were **inseparable**! And the adventures they had would fill a whole library of books. Like the time they trained a team of giant ants to carry away the logs Paul had chopped down … But that's another story!

A. Comprehension: Fact finding

Answer the questions.

1. What country does Paul Bunyan come from?
2. How does Paul clean his teeth?
3. What happened when baby Paul cried for the first time?
4. Why couldn't Paul make friends with other children?
5. What did Paul do to help Babe the first time they met?

Make up one more sentence describing the cold winter Paul met Babe.

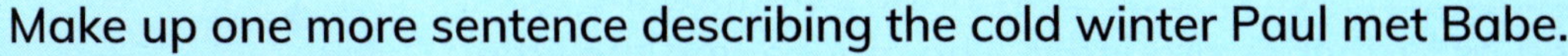

B. Comprehension: Read between the lines

Answer the questions.

1. Do you think this story is really true? Why or why not?
2. Why did Paul make such a good lumberjack?
3. What might have happened to Babe if Paul hadn't seen him?
4. Why do you think Paul and Babe became such good friends?
5. Which detail in this story do you think is funniest? Why?

Write the start of a story about when Paul and Babe trained the ants.

C. Vocabulary

Choose the word or phrase that is nearest in meaning to the underlined word.

1. Hercules was the <u>mightiest</u> hero in Greek mythology.
   a) strongest **b)** oldest **c)** naughtiest **d)** smallest
2. I sailed my speedboat on the pond but it <u>capsized</u>.
   a) overturned **b)** broke **c)** lost control **d)** drifted away
3. Dad <u>felled</u> the apple tree in our back garden.
   a) planted **b)** cut down **c)** pruned **d)** sprayed
4. A <u>glacial</u> wind was whistling down the street.
   a) strong **b)** icy **c)** roaring **d)** tropical
5. All I had for lunch was a <u>minute</u> sandwich.
   a) quick **b)** tasty **c)** nasty **d)** tiny
6. It's <u>toasty</u> in my bedroom on cold winter nights.
   a) freezing **b)** warm **c)** comfortable **d)** uncomfortable

Write sentences about the weather using 'glacial' and 'toasty'.

D. Vocabulary

Choose the most suitable words to complete the paragraph.

shivery inseparable mite drifted tumbled sapling

It was winter, and the little fir tree _______ stood alone as the snow _______ down. All of a sudden, a mouse _______ down the hill towards the tree. The mouse scrambled up the tree's trunk and hid in the branches. The little _______ was _______ with the cold, but the tree gathered its branches around it. The mouse and the little tree made friends, and before long they were _______.

Write more of the story using the words 'drifted' and 'sapling'.

E. Grammar: Adverbs (part 2)

We usually make **adverbs** by adding *-ly* to an adjective.
Example: quick + *-ly* = **quickly**
If the adjective ends in *-y*, replace y with i and add *-ly*.
Example: happy + *-ly* = **happily**

Change these adjectives into adverbs.

generous	lazy	innocent	grumpy
selfish	kind	brave	dangerous

Write the sentences, changing the adjectives into adverbs.

1. 'Thank you,' said Jamie (polite).
2. The children ran (happy) out into the playground.
3. The ogre stomped (angry) out of the cave.
4. The space ship landed (silent) on the grass.
5. Mara shook her head (slow).
6. Karen (wise) said nothing.

Choose three adverbs of your own and write sentences for them.

F. Writing skills: Describing atmosphere

The **atmosphere** is the **mood** of a story. The descriptive words you use in your story will decide what kind of mood it has.

Example: Words such as **'gloomy'**, **'misty'**, and **'chilling'** can help create a **spooky** mood.

Look at this picture of a spooky castle.

1. List at least six words and phrases that describe the picture.
2. Write the first few lines of a story set at the castle. Use words and phrases that will create a scary atmosphere.

G. Writing genre: Writing a fantasy narrative

Use the mind map you made in Unit 14a to write a fantasy story.

1. Write your first draft. Remember to:
   - Use adjectives, verbs and adverbs that will help the reader imagine the setting.
   - Use words and phrases that will give your story lots of atmosphere.
2. Ask a partner to read your story and give you feedback. Could they picture the setting? Could they feel the atmosphere?
3. Write your final draft, correcting any mistakes and making any improvements you can.

15a A Plant's Plea

Ouch! Watch it! This is the *third* time your football has taken off one of my leaves! I can see you love playing in the garden, but don't you ever think about us plants and our feelings?

What do you mean, you didn't think plants had feelings? Just because we can't talk – myself **excluded**, of course – that doesn't mean you can just **trample** all over us!

Listen, I know I probably just look like an **overgrown** weed to you. But actually, I'm a sunflower. Or I would be if you'd let me GROW! You know, I'm not that **demanding**. All I need is a bit of water from time to time and perhaps a nice feed of fertiliser. Then I'd put on a wonderful show in your garden all summer! I'd be taller than you in no time and my yellow petals would **blaze** out as brightly as the summer sun.

Perhaps you're wondering why I deserve to take up space in your garden. Maybe you think it would be better just to get rid of all the plants and clear the ground for a football pitch? But think about it! There are so many benefits to having plants like me in the garden. Let me draw your attention to just a few of them.

First of all, plants are fascinating. You can learn a lot from watching us grow. You'll see how we get bigger as we **gain** energy from sunlight, water and the delicious compost you give us. You'll watch us form flower buds that burst open to create a firework display of colour all summer long. And as autumn approaches, you'll see our seedheads form and ripen.

That brings me to another benefit. Plants like we sunflowers are brilliant for encouraging wildlife! Bees and butterflies love our **nectar**-filled flowers. And if you leave our seedheads in place as the seeds ripen, you'll encourage all kinds of birds and animals to your garden. You can enjoy the **acrobatics** of greenfinches, bluetits and robins as they visit to **gorge** on our ripe seeds. You might even see a squirrel trying to have a sneaky nibble!

So flowers like me are fascinating, beautiful and good for wildlife. What's not to love? Perhaps you think it'll be hard work looking after me and the other plants in your garden. But let me tell you a secret. Once you get started with gardening, you'll quickly become hooked. There's nothing to beat the feeling of watching plants you've **nurtured** from seeds as they bloom and grow!

What's more, once you discover the fun of growing things you can eat, you'll never look back. Did you know it's not only birds and small animals that can eat my seeds? Humans like you enjoy them too. All you have to do is slip them out of their shells for a nutty, chewy treat. I hear that they're even nicer roasted! Make sure you save a few seeds, though, so you can plant them. Then you'll have my **descendants** in your garden year after year!

But there's more to gardening than just flowers. There's a whole world of fruit and vegetables just waiting to be grown! Do you like juicy, sweet strawberries – or crisp, crunchy carrots? If you enjoy shop-bought fruit and vegetables, just wait till you've tried your own garden **produce**! The flavours are sharper and sweeter when you grow them yourself. It also means you can pick fruit and vegetables at the very peak of ripeness. Imagine the satisfaction of sitting in the garden eating a strawberry you've grown yourself, all sweet and warm from the sun!

So, by all means, keep on playing football. It's fun and good for you – or so I've been told. But make sure you don't kick and trample us plants! And you know it wouldn't kill you to put your football down occasionally and pick up a watering can. There's one over there, actually – look! If you fill it up at the water tap, you can give me a lovely cool drink. Ahhh! Thank you, that's better!

A. Comprehension: Fact finding

Answer the questions.

1. Who is speaking in *A Plant's Plea*?
2. What does a sunflower need to grow?
3. What happens to a sunflower as autumn gets closer?
4. What wild creatures eat sunflower seeds?
5. Name one advantage of growing your own food.

What makes this different from other persuasive texts?

B. Comprehension: Read between the lines

Answer the questions.

1. Why is the sunflower annoyed at the start of the text?
2. Why shouldn't the child eat all the sunflower seeds?
3. What is the best thing about growing sunflowers, in your opinion?
4. How do you think the child feels about plants by the end of the text?
5. Did this text persuade you to try gardening? Why or why not?

Write a reply to the plant's plea.

C. Vocabulary

Choose the word or phrase that is nearest in meaning to the underlined word.

1. Don't trample on Mr Carter's flower beds!
   a) dance **b)** lie **c)** sit **d)** tread
2. We watched fireworks blaze in the night sky.
   a) burn **b)** sizzle **c)** shine brightly **d)** grow
3. To gain respect from your teacher, always do your homework.
   a) get **b)** keep **c)** lose **d)** feel
4. In autumn, the birds gorge on berries in the hedgerows.
   a) sit **b)** nibble **c)** feed greedily **d)** live
5. Ali nurtured the tadpoles until they turned into frogs.
   a) cured **b)** looked after **c)** nursed **d)** cleaned
6. Jenny was sad because she felt excluded.
   a) included **b)** left out **c)** lonely **d)** involved

Five of the underlined words are verbs. Use one in a sentence.

15b It's Your Environment, So Get Involved!

Do you ever wonder who's in charge of **preserving** your local environment? Farmers and gardeners have a role to play. So do the **council** workers who look after the parks or empty our bins. But **ultimately**, it's up to all of us to take care of the environment. Children who are in primary school **currently** will be the grown-ups running the country in a **decade** or two! So it makes sense to help look after the environment now. That way, you can avoid causing problems that you'll just have to solve later.

Additionally, you can get lots of benefits from collaborating with others to improve the environment.

- You'll make friends and have fun as you get stuck in to projects like putting up bird feeders, making your school grounds wildlife-friendly, or planting trees in a nearby wood.
- You'll become an expert on local plants and animals.
- You'll get a real sense of satisfaction from doing something positive to improve the world around you.

You might be thinking, 'But I'm just a child! I can't do anything!' You might think you need special skills and experience to make a positive **impact** on your environment. But you'd be wrong! Anyone can help. All kinds of different skills and abilities are welcome. Here's a handy guide to activities that might suit you, depending on what you like doing best.

If you like being active ...

Help grown-ups to plant trees in a local wood, or ask your school if you can plant some in the school grounds.

Find a stream or pond that's **clogged** with rubbish. Ask permission to have a clearing party and get rid of all the rubbish. You'll need adult help for this!

Do a sponsored run or swim to raise money for a local environmental project. Check noticeboards, the local paper and the internet to find out what's going on locally.

If you like being crafty ...

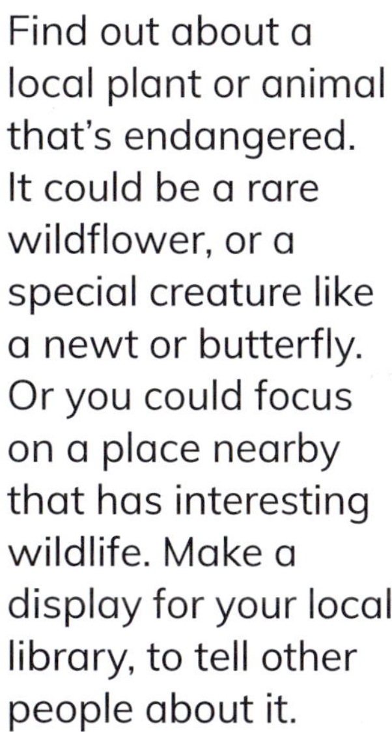

Find out about a local plant or animal that's endangered. It could be a rare wildflower, or a special creature like a newt or butterfly. Or you could focus on a place nearby that has interesting wildlife. Make a display for your local library, to tell other people about it.

Ask friends and relatives to give you junk that they would otherwise throw away or recycle. See how much rubbish you can collect. Then use all the rubbish to make a giant **sculpture** to display at school. Add a sign reminding everyone not to drop litter!

Make a poster for your classroom, to **encourage** everyone to look after garden birds or small mammals such as hedgehogs.

If you like animals and birds ...

Make a bird feeder by packing some lard and birdseeds into an old yoghurt pot, and hanging it up in the garden. Watch and see how many different birds come to eat from it!

Encourage hedgehogs to come into your garden by asking a grown-up to make sure there are gaps in the fence they can get through. Put out some tinned cat food (not the fishy sort) and **ensure** there's some fresh water for them to drink.

Build a bug hotel by making a bundle of **hollow** sticks which insects can crawl into. This will help them survive when the autumn and winter come.

There's no limit to the ways you can help the environment in your local area – all you need is a little imagination. So what are you waiting for? Get started today!

A. Comprehension: Fact finding

Answer the questions.

1. Name a job that involves looking after the environment.
2. List two things you can do if you enjoy being active.
3. What could you do to help garden birds?
4. What sort of food should you *not* give to hedgehogs?
5. Name two things listed in the text that you can do without adult help.

Do you agree children should help look after the environment? Give reasons.

B. Comprehension: Read between the lines

Answer the questions.

1. What is the main purpose of this text?
2. Name an activity that informs others about the environment.
3. Why do you think the author includes so many different activities?
4. Which idea would work best with a large group of children? Why?
5. Does this text make you want to help the environment? Why?

Which of the ideas in this piece would suit you best? Give reasons.

C. Vocabulary

Choose the word or phrase that is nearest in meaning to the underlined word.

1. I am <u>currently</u> saving for a new phone.
   a) really **b)** recently **c)** hopefully **d)** now
2. We saw an amazing tropical plant that only blooms once every <u>decade</u>.
   a) hundred years **b)** ten years **c)** few months **d)** fifty days
3. Always wear a helmet when skateboarding, and <u>additionally</u> kneepads.
   a) unfortunately **b)** definitely **c)** also **d)** despite this
4. Siobhán's beautiful voice had a powerful <u>impact</u> on the audience.
   a) effect **b)** loss **c)** experience **d)** understanding
5. The gutters overflowed because the drain was <u>clogged</u> with leaves.
   a) decorated **b)** blocked **c)** scattered **d)** flooded
6. Teresa made an amazing <u>sculpture</u> out of milk cartons.
   a) artwork **b)** picture **c)** object **d)** model

Use 'currently' in a sentence about what you are doing right now.

D. Vocabulary

Choose the most suitable word to complete each sentence.

preserving ultimately council encourage hollow ensure

1. The _______ workers keep the streets tidy and clean.
2. _______ the environment isn't difficult – anyone can help!
3. We can all help _______ that school is a happy place.
4. _______, it's our responsibility to take care of the environment.
5. The owl looked out at us from inside the _______ tree.
6. Selina made a display to _______ people to look after hedgehogs.

Write sentences for two of the words from the box.

E. Grammar: Dictionary skills

Dictionaries help you find the **definition** (meaning) and correct **spelling** of a word. Dictionaries show words in **alphabetical order**.

We work out alphabetical order by looking at the first letter in a word, then the second letter, and so on.

Example: ant, anteater, antelope, bear, beetle, camel, caterpillar.

Write each of the four groups of words in alphabetical order.

- crossroads, copper, crow, cracker
- phone, phantom, pile, purple
- necklace, nothing, night, nectarine
- magnet, military, mackerel, magic

Find these words in a dictionary. Write their definitions.

- tedious
- province
- clammy
- shingle
- brandish
- fungus

Choose a text in this book. List any words you don't know. Find them in a dictionary.

F. Writing skills: Facts and opinions

Facts give evidence for a point of view. Facts are always true.

Opinions help persuade the reader to think the same way you do.

Persuasive texts often use a mix of facts and opinions.

Examples:

- **Fact** – Numbers of butterflies are going down in Ireland.
- **Opinion** – We should grow plants that butterflies like, to help them.

Read the sentences and write whether each is a fact or an opinion.

1. Foxes often scavenge food from dustbins.
2. Foxes are horrible animals.
3. Chickens can make great pets.
4. Chickens usually lay one egg per day.
5. Strawberries are high in Vitamin C.
6. Strawberries are absolutely delicious!

Choose one of these animals. Write one fact and one opinion about it.

badger

swan

deer

G. Writing genre: Writing a persuasive article

Use the plan you made in Unit 15a to write a persuasive article.

1. Write your first draft. Remember to:
   - Address the reader directly
   - Give your opinions clearly
   - Use a mix of facts and your opinions to make your argument convincing
   - Use informal and persuasive words and phrases
   - Finish with a conclusion that summarises what you want the reader to do and why.
2. Edit your article, making any improvements needed.
3. Write your final draft.

D. Vocabulary – revision

Choose the most suitable word to complete each sentence.

bland slammed escaped hurtling donation congested

1. The tiger ________ from his cage.
2. The heavy metal door ________ shut behind me.
3. In the morning the roads are ________ with cars.
4. I made a ________ to a charity that protects wild elephants.
5. I like spicy food but my sister prefers ________ food.
6. The cheetah went ________ through the desert at lightning speed.

Write one sentence using three words from the box.

E. Grammar: Revision – verbs

Write these verbs in the past tense. Be careful – some of them are irregular!

jump prance walk zip run jog slide swim

Rewrite the sentences so that the verbs agree with the subjects.

1. Jenny were happy to see us.
2. The swans swims calmly down the river.
3. My favourite type of music are rap.
4. We always eats a cooked breakfast on Sundays.
5. The boys is sitting on the wall.
6. We is glad it's nearly dinner time.

Think of a more interesting verb to replace each underlined one.

1. 'Don't be silly!' said Mam.
2. The boys ate their lunch.
3. Jessica likes chocolate biscuits.
4. 'I don't want to go for a walk!' I said.
5. The cheetah ran after the gazelle.
6. Grandpa was sleeping in the armchair.

Imagine a monster joins in with your PE lesson. Use interesting verbs to describe what the monster does.

F. Writing skills: Word effects – alliteration and rhyme

Poems often use words with interesting **sounds** that go well together when read aloud. When words that are close together *start* with the same sound, it's called **alliteration**.

Example: The owl swooped and swished softly past.

Write the sentences and circle the alliteration.

1. The wind whistled and wailed through the woods.
2. The snake slithered slyly over the sand.
3. The magnificent moon made the moment seem magic.
4. The fat frog flopped across the frozen pond.

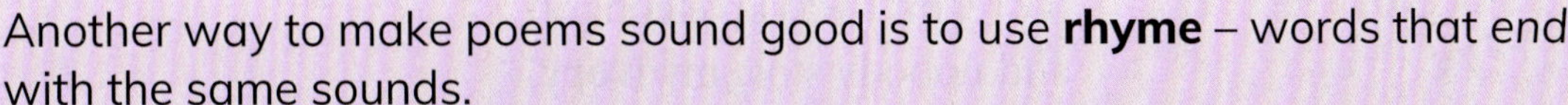

Another way to make poems sound good is to use **rhyme** – words that end with the same sounds.

Example: Gardens full of plants and trees
Are good for butterflies and bees.

Find and write three pairs of rhyming words from 'Blake's Tyger – Revisited'.

Sort these words into rhyming pairs. You could use some of them in a short poem about nature.

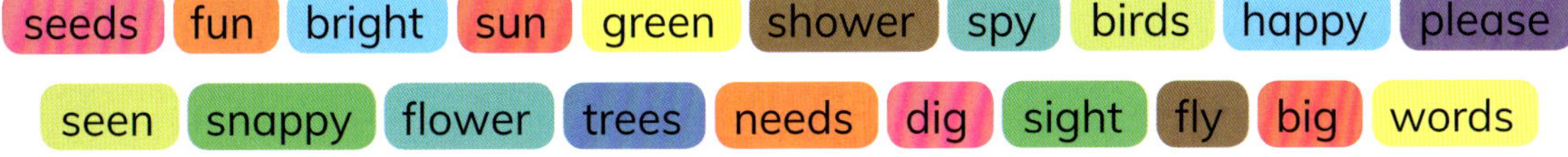

G. Writing genre: Planning a poem with interesting sounds

Plan a poem with alliteration, rhyme, or both!

1. Choose an animal, bird, fish or insect that you would like to write about.
2. Make a mind map of words and phrases that describe:
   - What the creature looks like
   - Where it lives
   - How it moves
   - What it might be thinking or feeling.
3. Think about alliteration and rhyme and add:
   - Words with the same sounds at the start
   - Rhyming pairs of words.

16b Dreamer

I dreamt I was an ocean
and no one **polluted** me.

I dreamt I was a whale
and no **hunters chased** after me.

I dreamt I was the air
and nothing **blackened** me.

I dreamt I was a stream
and nobody **poisoned** me.

I dreamt I was an elephant
and nobody stole my **ivory**.

I dreamt I was a rainforest
and no one cut down my trees.

I dreamt I painted a smile
on the face of the earth
for all to see.

Brian Moses

A. Comprehension: Fact finding

Answer the questions.

1. What animals does the poet dream of being?
2. What problem might an ocean have, according to the poem?
3. Why might people hunt elephants?
4. What problem might a rainforest have?
5. How is the last verse different from the rest?

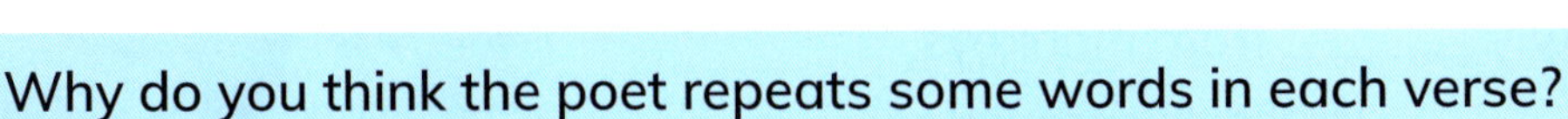

Why do you think the poet repeats some words in each verse?

B. Comprehension: Read between the lines

Answer the questions.

1. What do the things the poet dreams about have in common?
2. Do you think this poem is about happy or sad dreams? Why?
3. Reread verse three. What might 'blacken' the air?
4. Which verse of the poem do you like best? Why?
5. How does this poem make you feel? Why?

What is the main message of this poem? Explain why you think this.

C. Vocabulary

Choose the word or phrase that is nearest in meaning to the underlined word.

1. The sea was polluted with waste and rubbish.
   a) filled **b)** contaminated **c)** awash **d)** miserable
2. The boys chased the dog around the field.
   a) sent **b)** watched **c)** ran with **d)** pursued
3. The stream was poisoned, so there were no fish in it.
   a) dirty **b)** polluted **c)** dried up **d)** smelly
4. Ivory is highly prized by hunters.
   a) leather **b)** cream **c)** wood **d)** animal bones or tusks
5. After the fire, the house was completely blackened.
   a) destroyed **b)** charred **c)** ruined **d)** burnt out
6. Hunters stalked their prey through the jungle.
   a) trackers **b)** thieves **c)** settlers **d)** fighters

Find two words that mean nearly the same thing. Use them in a sentence.

D. Vocabulary – revision

Choose the most suitable word to complete each sentence.

chaos collaborated nurtured loathe serenely evolved

1. The toddler's birthday party was total ______!
2. The swan glided ______ across the lake.
3. My friend and I ______ on our science project.
4. Humans slowly ______ from monkeys.
5. I absolutely ______ Brussels sprouts!
6. The vet carefully ______ the sick animals.

Write dictionary definitions for two of the words from the box.

E. Grammar: Revision – adjectives and adverbs

Draw the table below. Put the words from the boxes in the correct columns.

hairy little magically slowly green wearily

fresh hopeful perfectly coolly silly

Adjectives	Adverbs
beautiful	*quickly*

Write the comparative form of these adjectives.

hard nice heavy light lovely hot near fast

These adjectives have irregular comparatives. Write them down. Look them up in a dictionary if you're not sure!

far little bad good

Choose one of the comparative adjectives above and use it in a sentence.

Write adjectives you could use to describe the nouns in the first line of each verse of 'Dreamer'.

F. Writing skills: Word choices – synonyms

Choosing the right descriptive words will help the reader to picture in their mind what you are writing about. A **thesaurus** can help you find **synonyms** (words with similar meanings) for common words.

Write the sentences. Use a thesaurus to find more interesting synonyms for the underlined words.

1. It was a cold day.
2. I ate my dinner very quickly.
3. We went to school as fast as we could.
4. Bella skipped along happily.
5. Jamie shrugged his shoulders sadly.

Improve this description by using more powerful synonyms for the underlined words.

It was a hot day. I went outside to water the flowers. There was one small blue flower. It had small blue petals and big leaves. It was pretty, but it was wilting. I quickly gave it some water. It seemed happy then!

G. Writing genre: Writing a poem with interesting sounds

Use the mind map you made in Unit 16a to write a poem with interesting sounds.

1. Write your first draft.
2. Read your first draft out loud. Can you:
   - Add more alliteration or other rhyming pairs of words about your chosen animal?
   - Improve any of them by using more interesting synonyms?
3. Read your poem to a partner and ask them for feedback.
4. Write a final draft of your poem, adding an illustration of the animal your poem is about.

You could put all your poems in a class book of animal poetry!

Acknowledgements

The author and Publisher wish to thank the following for permission to reproduce copyright material:

Pp. 42-44 *Letting Go* by Kerri Ward. © Kerri Ward; pp. 48–50 Extract from *The Fastest Boy in the World* by Elizabeth Laird, published with permission of Macmillan Children's Books, an imprint of Pan Macmillan, a division of Macmillan Publishers International Limited. © 2014 Elizabeth Laird; p. 90 'The Wind' by Gareth Owen. Published by Young Lions, 1988. © Gareth Owen. Reproduced by permission of the author c/o Rogers, Coleridge & White Ltd., 20 Powis Mews, London W11 1JN; pp. 78–80 *On the Trail of Ded Moroz* by Kieran Fanning. © Kieran Fanning; pp 84–86 *A Light in the Window* by Catherine Baker. © Catherine Baker; p. 94 'Weather' by Eve Merriam. From *Catch a Little Rhyme* by Eve Merriam. © 1966 Eve Merriam. © Renewed 1994. Used by permission of Marian Reiner; pp. 122–124 Extract from *Under the Hawthorn Tree* by Marita Conlon-McKenna published by The O'Brien Press Ltd, Dublin. © Marita Conlon-McKenna; pp. 128–130 Extract from *Cherokee* by Creina Mansfield published by The O'Brien Press Ltd, Dublin. © Creina Mansfield; pp. 158–160 Extract from *Matilda* by Roald Dahl, published by Penguin Books Ltd. © The Roald Dahl Story Company Limited; p. 182 'Blake's Tyger – Revisited' by Michaela Morgan. © Michaela Morgan; p. 186 'Dreamer' by Brian Moses. © Brian Moses. All rights reserved.